*

Dialogue with Death

*

Dialogue with Death

A JOURNEY INTO
CONSCIOUSNESS

*by Eknath
Easwaran*

Nilgiri Press

I S B N : cloth, 0–915132–73–7; paper, 0–915132–72–9

Second edition, first printing November 1992

The Blue Mountain Center of Meditation,
founded by Eknath Easwaran
in Berkeley, California, in 1961,
publishes books on how to lead
the spiritual life in the home
and the community.

For information please write to
Nilgiri Press, Box 256,
Tomales, California 94971

Printed on recycled, permanent paper

The paper used in this publication meets the minimum
requirements of American National Standard for Information Services –
Permanence of Paper for Printed Library Materials,
ANSI Z39.48–1984

Library of Congress Cataloging-in-Publication data
will be found on the last page of this book.

Table of Contents

TO CHRISTINE

Preface

I am gratified to hear that the first edition of this book has brought strength and understanding to those who are facing death, whether their own or of one they are caring for. But *Dialogue with Death* is not really a book on death and dying. It is a book about life and living: what life is for, who we are as human beings, why we are here.

Yet it is death that forces these questions on us. If we could live forever, there would be little urgency in finding answers. But the fact is that whatever our age or the status of our health, none of us has time to waste in learning what life is for.

In this sense, then, death is a friend – not the clinical experience of dying, but the fact of our mortality. We begin to take life seriously when we take death seriously. Otherwise, as Thoreau said, we run the risk of discovering, when we come to die, that we have never lived.

This is not a negative observation. It is completely positive, for it brings life into focus. Every moment is precious; each day should be full of meaning. Once we grasp this, we find there is no time to squander on anger or depression, no time for quarreling with those we love. Fulfilling the purpose of life becomes our overriding priority, and that brings joy, hope, love, and meaning to us and to those around us.

In a biological sense, each of us is engaged continuously in a dialogue with death. The processes of life and death proceed together from the moment we are conceived. And of course, there comes a time when life begins to lose ground. At that point, as far as biology goes, we enter the second half of life, a losing battle in which most of us hope for little more than to slow the advance of time.

But there is another sense of this phrase "the second half of life," which has little to do with age. In this view, the first part merely sets the stage for the drama we are born to play. This is the time for experimentation, when we play with life's toys – money, pleasure, power, possessions, prestige – and learn for ourselves what they are worth.

Many people never go beyond this phase. Nothing in modern civilization, with its cult of youth, encourages us to look farther. But it is only when we throw these toys away and begin to search for answers to those essential questions – *Who am I? Why am I here? What is life for?* – that we really begin to live.

For these are the years in which each of us is meant to grow to our full stature as a human being. They are the years when profound personal discoveries and great contributions are made, which can only come when a person turns inward. For those who take up this challenge, life holds out unique promise: the fulfillment of living for a lofty goal, and of finally discovering within themselves a living presence that is beyond change and death.

Of course, this is just the opposite of what the world believes. The media saturate us with the message that only youth and material possessions make life worthwhile. But it is my experience that many young people today have already discovered that physical satisfactions cannot satisfy the hunger in their hearts. They know that life must have more to offer, and that they are meant for much bigger things.

India's spiritual tradition tells of several young men and women like this. One, a teenage boy named Nachiketa, goes to the King of Death himself to find the answers to his questions. His story – another kind of dialogue with Death, complete with this unique teacher's spiritual instruction – is told in an ancient text called the Katha Upanishad, which is the origin of this book. Most of the material in these pages began with a series of talks I gave to a very earnest, intimate group – mostly students in their twenties – who were one of the best audiences I have ever had. Like Nachiketa, they burned with the desire to know who they are and why they are here. The Katha made a perfect guide for the inner journey we took together in search of answers.

As a boy, I was terribly afraid of death. In village India, as you must know, the dying are not hidden away behind institutional walls. Death is woven into our lives, and the deathbed scenes I witnessed as a child filled me with terror. It was my spiritual teacher, my grandmother, who showed me how I could use that terror to focus all the energies of my life on Self-realization.

Today, in my eighties, death holds no fear for me. For today I know – not merely believe but *know*, as each of us can know – that death is only a door, and dying no more than a change of rooms. And I look on death as a friend, for it has taught me to live completely in the present, full of faith and free from fear.

This realization is the goal of life: not an end but a beginning. No pursuit can be more rewarding. In this sense, this book is an invitation to a journey that every one of us was born to make. I warmly encourage you to join me!

EKNATH EASWARAN

DIALOGUE WITH DEATH

Chapter One

An Inward Journey

L ET ME START with a story – one that
has been handed down for thousands of
years. Its hero is a teenager in ancient India named Nachiketa, who
goes to the King of Death to learn the meaning of life. The place is
not essential to the narrative, but Nachiketa's age is not incidental.
Teenagers can show tremendous spiritual potential, for they have
the passion, the desire, the idealism, and the reckless daring to stake
everything they have on an almost impossible goal.

Nachiketa has this daring, and he has also one other characteristic of teenagers that can get them into a lot of trouble: he is a ruthless
observer. He sees right through superficial behavior, and like the
little boy in the story of the emperor's new clothes, he calls a spade
a spade.

The opening scene is timeless; I can imagine it in Berkeley or
Boston as easily as in ancient India. Nachiketa's father is a real pillar of the community. He has wealth and status and everybody looks

up to him, probably not without a twinge of envy. But as can sometimes happen to community pillars, he has grown accustomed to
making compromises with his values. When the story opens, he has
decided to make a grand donation to a worthy charity: the temple
building fund. And a familiar little voice seems to have whispered,
"Wouldn't you like to have your name on the cornerstone of that
temple? Wouldn't it be pleasant to hear the priest announce, 'Without Nachiketa Senior, this magnificent edifice would never have
been built. Generations to come will bless his name'?" So
Nachiketa's father announces grandly that he is giving away all his
possessions for this noble purpose – including a large herd of
cows, which were legal tender in ancient India. And everyone is
duly impressed.

Everyone, that is, except Nachiketa. "Dad," he protests in a loud
whisper, "what do you mean by that? You're not giving away all
your possessions! All you're donating is a lot of cows, most of them
on their last legs. They're so old they can scarcely see, scarcely
even walk; if they put their heads down to graze, they might never
get them up again. Who's going to praise you for a gift like that?"

Nachiketa's father is hurt and embarrassed; he pretends not to
hear. But Nachiketa is not any readier than most teenagers to pass
off his father's behavior with a shrug. "Dad," he says, "am I your
possession? Why don't you give me away too?"

His father bites back an angry reply.

"Well, Dad?"

Still no answer, though his father is fuming. But the boy persists.
"Are you going to give me to the temple, Dad?"

And finally his father explodes. "I'll give you to Death!"

The words are only an expression of anger, like our modern
equivalent: "Drop dead!" The man is furious; his vision is clouded
over by passion, and he lashes out with thoughtless words.

But Nachiketa is not angry, and his eyes are clear. He sees these
uncontrolled, unconscious forces erupt into his father's usually loving behavior, and the sight plunges him into reflection. "Does he
mean that? Would he really send me to Death? Can a father's love be

blown away by a passing storm? . . . And what about those cows? He is a good man, yet even he can close his eyes to what is right."

Most of us have experienced moments when one isolated incident – a chance encounter, a near-fatal accident, the death of someone we love, even a tragedy read about in the morning paper – suddenly brings into sharp focus the central questions of existence. *Why am I here? What happens after death? How ought I to live?* We turn inwards in reflection; but if we cannot go deep into ourselves, the surface pattern of everyday living soon closes in again and the questions are forgotten.

For Nachiketa, however, the moment of questioning does not pass. A trap door has opened in his consciousness. He is only sixteen or so; probably he has never thought much about death before. But now he begins to ponder what it would mean to die – not as an abstract fancy, but as if he were to be snatched away by death that very day.

"Look at those who have gone before us," Nachiketa wonders. "Millions on millions – men, women, and children. Where have they gone?" Which of us has not asked this question, in those rare moments when the veil of superficial vision is held aside? T. S. Eliot, I remember, watches the crowds pass over London Bridge all faceless and nameless in the morning fog – coming from nowhere, going nowhere – and suddenly sees the passage from this world to the next. London disappears; he is Dante, standing at the edge of the river Styx on his way to the land of the dead. "So many! I had not thought death had undone so many." Nachiketa too now looks around and asks, "Is it the same for us?" We know the answer, though we seldom act as if we knew it: "All that live must die." As the Bible says, "All flesh is grass." We come up, flourish a while, and then – so soon! – like grass in the dead heat of summer, we are gone.

For what end? Have our lives no more significance than grass does? So brief life seems when it is over, and for many of us, so futile! "We are such stuff as dreams are made on," Shakespeare says – growing up, going to school, getting married, begetting children, getting and spending, growing old – "and our little life is rounded with a sleep," before we even open our eyes to find out who we are.

"Is that all?" Nachiketa asks. "No more to life than that?" Nothing to do but enjoy each day for what it offers – a few good meals, a friend or two, some pleasant memories and unlikely hopes – and then make our exit without fuss or fanfare? Or is there more, a secret that few dream of and even fewer try to find?

"I give you to Death!" Thoughtless, angry words, but they have opened a door deep into Nachiketa's heart. Superficial living will not satisfy him any longer. He must know if there is a purpose to life, to *his* life, and he must learn it from the most knowledgeable teacher he can find. "I will go to Death," he resolves: "but not as others go, never to return. I will go to Death to learn the meaning of life."

The Land of Death

Except for one essential difference, we might still be in any teenager's home in Berkeley or Boston: Nachiketa now leaves home to find his purpose in life. The difference is that this is not an external journey; it all takes place within.

In Hindu mythology, I should explain, there is a great deal of personification. Forces of nature and of the mind are represented as gods, goddesses, and demons; states of consciousness become unearthly realms. So Death is personified as Yama, the Controller, for it is he who administers the central law of the phenomenal world: that all of nature is in continuous change, and therefore whatever comes into existence, whether it is a microbe, a human being, or a star, must someday pass away. Whenever the seasons change, when moths are swept away by a storm, when the thread of a human relationship is cut, Yama is administering his law. In more modern language he is an eternal force, and therefore Nachiketa counts him among the "ageless immortals" who have gone beyond death and change. Similarly, when Nachiketa descends to the Land of Death, his destination is not some place beneath the earth. Death and his kingdom are right inside us all.

As a student of English literature, I must have read dozens of novels in which the hero went off somewhere "in search of himself." Often the search for meaning does start with a sense of restlessness, which can carry us all over the earth. But sooner or later every serious student of life sets aside passport and visas and settles down to look within.

There is a vast world waiting. The outer world has boundaries, but the mind is boundless; time and space have very little meaning in its realms. I do not think anything makes a better comparison than the sea. Its surface too is constantly changing and opaque; yet deep below the surface are mountains larger than the Himalayas, great gorges deeper than the Grand Canyon, creatures that spend their lives where light has never penetrated. This may be a poetic view of the unconscious, but it is not at all inaccurate.

Oceanographers have learned to wrap a little part of the surface world in metal and descend deep into the sea, to seek out its secrets with instruments and searchlights. The descent into the mind is no less scientific. The vehicle, if I may call it that, is meditation, by which we take the light of consciousness gradually deeper and deeper until the whole of the mind is illumined from surface to seabed.

Today the word *meditation* is used to mean all sorts of things: letting the mind drift, dancing, playing music, even running. I want to make it very clear that when I talk about meditation, I use the word only in the precise, traditional sense of a dynamic discipline by which all the powers of the mind are brought together into a single-pointed focus. The same practice appears, under different names, in all the major spiritual traditions of the world, and the method I have found effective in my own experience would be recognized by mystics anywhere.

I have given full instructions in meditation in other books, so there is no need to go into details here. But some broad outlines will

make it easier to illustrate in later pages what happens within the
mind as meditation deepens.

The mind is essentially a process, a flow of thoughts. The faster
and more turbulent this flow is, the harder it is to go below the surface level of awareness into the unconscious realms where our desires and fears, problems and aspirations arise. In meditation, we
teach the mind to go slowly with concentration through the words
of a passage that embodies the highest of spiritual ideals. In this way
we can gradually slow down the furious rush of thought, giving increasing self-mastery. Finally, in the climax of meditation, we discover the real core of our personality, which the Hindu scriptures
call simply *Atman* – our real Self.

This is a long, arduous, and terribly challenging endeavor, as I
think the chapters that follow will make clear. It is not the work of
days but of many years. But Nachiketa has an almost unheard-of
singleness of purpose. When he sits down and closes his eyes in
meditation, he drops into the very depths of consciousness, like a
diver penetrating those fathomless realms where light has never entered. Here, according to the theory of reincarnation, the experience of death is written over and over in the unconscious, perhaps a
million times. This is the Land of Death: the last frontier between
death and immortality, between the perishable individual personality and the imperishable Self.

Ironically, however, the King is not at home. His servants –
Pestilence, War, Famine, Depression, and so on – are in conster-
nation. Nobody has come looking for Death as far back as they can
remember. Depression just stammers with embarrassment, "He's
out." Death is a busy man. He can't stay around at home and read.
He has tremendous demands on his time and energy: places to go,
appointments to meet. "He hardly ever comes home any more,"
War complains; "he just phones in for messages. He's a real Type A
personality, always on the run."

But this self-possessed teenager is not one to be turned away. He
sits down quietly and says, "I'll wait" – a day, a month, a year,

however long it takes. He has come too far to turn back empty-handed.

It is said that the Buddha, after six or seven years of searching, sat down in meditation with the resolve not to rise again until he had found the Eternal in this very life. Nachiketa is made of the same stuff. He waits in the realm of Death for three days and three nights – remember, this is in meditation – without food, without water, without sleep. And at the end of those three days and nights, he comes face to face with Death himself.

Yama's henchmen hasten to explain his presence. "He has come as your guest, and no ordinary guest either. To watch him in meditation you'd think he was a pillar of flame. Receive him with hospitality, O King! A guest is sacred, and this boy has come for some purpose for which he will not be defeated."

Death is not used to social amenities, but Nachiketa has already captured his interest. "You're young," he thinks to himself, "but you have the daring of one in a million million. What mission are you really on?"

Then he speaks aloud. "Young man," he says, "I have been a poor host. Please let me give you three boons, to atone for the three days and nights I have kept you waiting in this inhospitable realm."

The First Boon: Forgiveness

Surprisingly, perhaps, the first boon that Nachiketa asks is not really for himself but for his father. "O King, let my father's heart be free from anger. When I return from this land, may he rejoice to see me just as he did when I was born."

Look at the eyes of any parents when their first child arrives; it is the center of their whole world. How many times does a mother stay up with her infant? – not the way people sometimes stay up to meet a deadline, with moaning and groaning and a lot of pep pills, but with love. Most parents were like this once; most of us were cherished above everything else in the world.

Now comes the cruel question: for how long? As children grow into individuals with their own ideas and begin to go their separate ways, very few of us can continue to support them with the all-consuming, unfaltering love we gave when they were born.

So Yama promises: "Your home shall be as it was then. When you return from the Land of Death, your father will see you again as his very own, 'bone of his bone, life of his life.' I will set your father's heart at peace, and there will be no more estrangement between you."

Actually, there is great practical wisdom in this first boon. Without an all-forgiving compassion in our hearts, the gates to deepest consciousness can never open. No matter who has wronged us or how seriously we have been wronged, there should be no rancor in our hearts when we come face to face with death; it will divide us against ourselves.

The Second Boon: The Fire of Life

Nachiketa has set his house in order. His personal relationships are restored, and he is at peace with the world. Now, with cool detachment, he begins to take on Death in earnest. He gives Yama that quizzical look that teenagers give someone who knows an answer but might not give it, and he goes straight to the point.

"I have heard from the wise," he says, "that there is a kingdom, a state of consciousness, in which one lives free from the ravages of age and lives in ever-present vitality. They say you know a fire sacrifice that leads to this realm, O Death. Teach me that sacrifice as my second boon."

This sacrifice is not an external ritual. The fire Nachiketa refers to is the fire of life itself, called *prana* in Sanskrit. The word is often translated as "breath," for there is a close connection. But prana is much more basic than any vital function, and it is not physical. When it is present the heart can beat, the lungs can breathe, the brain can interpret signals and translate decisions into action. When prana is absent, though the vital organs may still be intact, life is gone. Formerly there was a living person; now there is only a body.

Fire is a perfect symbol for prana, because where prana is abundant, there *is* fire – intense enthusiasm, vitality, drive, resoluteness, the capacity to see something through right to the end without being distracted from the goal. Those who have this kind of fire can achieve anything they choose.

Swami Vivekananda remarked in this connection that some people are like dry tinder. You can set them on fire easily, but the fire is over almost as soon as it starts. It is a stinging observation, but an accurate one. If you want a fire, you cannot get far with nothing but tinder; you have to have some bigger stuff. And Vivekananda added, a few people are like big logs. You strike match after match and for the longest time everything just fizzles out. But once they do catch fire, they blaze as bright as any sun, and they do not burn out. These are the few – the very few, people like Mahatma Gandhi or Teresa of Avila – who manage to get hold of the source of prana and ignite it forever. Even after their bodies are gone, their lives continue to fire the enthusiasm of those who come after them, without being in any way diminished by time.

"Let me be like that!" Nachiketa tells Yama. "I don't want to be like everybody else, burning out after a few decades. Give me the sacrifice that is the secret of vitality, so that I can blaze like an eternal sun."

Even today, orthodox Hindus observe a ritual in which fire is produced by rubbing one firestick against another, just as it must have been done thousands of years ago. But this kind of ceremony is only a symbol. The sacrifice Death describes does not take place at the physical level. Inner fire is ignited by rubbing together two inner firesticks: one is the will; the other, our selfish passions and desires. Physical passions, especially sexual, are like fuel in a Ferrari. When such passions come under control of the will, immense vitality is at our fingertips – no longer just the usual supply of prana, but an unlimited reserve in a highly condensed form called *kundalini*. As a laser is radiation concentrated into an intense beam, kundalini is intensely concentrated prana, packed away until we are ready to draw on it.

For most human beings, this reserve lies hidden and dormant.

For kundalini is the fuel we require to complete the long, arduous journey of Self-realization. Until we begin this journey in earnest, to keep us from frittering it away on other pursuits, kundalini cannot be released. But when at last we begin to live for a higher purpose than ourselves, it is as if an intense fire is ignited deep in our consciousness, inflaming our enthusiasm and determination. As we draw on it more and more to make progress, this fire grows until it transfigures our personality.

Most of us, even if we desire it, take a long, long time to dedicate ourselves completely to such a goal. But Nachiketa does not hesitate. He is already at the deepest levels of consciousness; when Yama grants the boon, the boy is able to follow his instructions completely and offer all his personal desires to the fire within. Like young Thérèse of Lisieux he can truthfully say, "There is only one desire in all my heart" – the desire for Self-realization. It is such a simple statement that we can altogether miss the near impossibility of what it stands for, the sacrifice it requires, the immense power it releases from within.

Even Yama is impressed. But, like a good teacher, he scarcely shows it. With a show of casualness, he waits to administer the final test. The boy now has unlimited will and vitality in his hands. Will he waver in his destination? "Nachiketa, ask me now for your third boon."

The Third Boon: Immortality

Nachiketa does not beat around the bush. "I want the secret of life and death," he says, "and I have come straight to you to get it. When you cut off a man's life, where does he go? Is that the end, or is there something that you cannot slay? If that is the end, I want to know for certain. But if it is possible to go beyond death, show me the way. Teach me the truth; I am your student."

Death is pleased merely to hear this question asked. He meets a lot of people in the course of his work, yet very few care to learn anything from him. "In the mortal world," he would complain, "everybody wants a spectacle." To draw a crowd, you have to offer free

Frisbees and show up with a group of rock musicians wearing buffalo horns on their heads and dressed like abominable snowmen. If someone explains quietly how to challenge death, a few may come and enjoy the talk, but only one or two will be ready to come up afterwards and say, "How do I start?"

I can almost see the King of Death smiling behind his grisly palm and thinking, "Just the kind of pupil I want! " But first, of course, the boy has to pass his final exam to make sure he has the capacity and the dedication to graduate. Death is busy; he cannot waste time with second-rate students who are going to drop out after one or two years.

"Nachiketa," he says cleverly, "you're still rather young. Lots of older and wiser people have asked this question before you – philosophers, poets, theologians, scientists. If you like, you can read what they have to say about death. Leave it to them, Nachiketa; don't come to me."

Then he goes on to whet the boy's appetite. "Besides, Nachiketa, it's terribly difficult. I don't think you'd be able to make it."

That, of course, is just what teenagers like to hear. If Yama had said, "Sure, just take my postal correspondence course; six easy lessons or your life cheerfully refunded," the boy would not have taken him seriously.

"Death," he says – not "Your Highness," not even "O King," just "Death" – "the harder the better. There is no other ruler over death than you, and no other boon that I want than this."

"Don't underestimate," Death warns. "The path is sharp as a razor's edge. You have to have superhuman endurance, superhuman dedication; otherwise you cannot succeed. Nachiketa, why don't you ask for something else? Something within your reach. Be reasonable. Don't badger me any more about death; let me give you what you really want."

Nachiketa is about to open his mouth, but Yama reads the look in the boy's eyes. "Wait," he objects, holding up his hand. "You haven't heard my offer."

"All right," Nachiketa replies. "Let me see what you think I'm worth."

"First," Death says, "you can have as many sons and grandsons as you like." It is a rather sophisticated offer, because to have unlimited progeny, you have to have plenty of virility and ample opportunities to indulge it. So Yama pauses to let the implications sink in. Then he adds, "And wealth too. Cows enough to make your father's head swim, race horses, elephants, whatever you want."

Nachiketa starts to object, but Death holds up his hand. "No strings attached." An elephant, as everyone in India knows, eats an incredible amount. That is why they make such good status symbols for maharajas: if you're not rich, even one elephant can eat you out of house and home. So Yama adds, "All these animals come with the money it takes to feed them. And plenty of land too, as much of the earth as you want, so you won't get claustrophobia." Death has thought of everything.

And more. "How long do you want to live, Nachiketa? A couple of centuries? Why not more? Everlasting vitality goes with the deal too." If modern medicine could make an offer like that, the world would stand in line and say, "Oh, thank you, Death! " But Nachiketa just stands there contemptuously as if to say, "Is that all? Centuries more of unfulfilled existence? At the end, won't you still come to take us away?"

"If none of this is exactly what you want," Yama goes on casually, "ask for anything you like. Whatever it is, I will give it to you – along with enough money and a long, long life to enjoy whatever you choose. Give me a complete catalog of desires and I'll give you a complete catalog of satisfactions. Any pleasure you like – sensate, transient, what does it matter? Even if they are fleeting you can still have a lot of them. If you want a five-minute pleasure, ask for twelve an hour. Multiply that by twenty-four and you can fill up a day and night."

Then Death plays his ace. "Perhaps, Nachiketa, you're still a little young to understand what pleasures to choose. Probably your dad hasn't let you run about much; your mom has kept you tied to her sari strings. Is it hard to imagine? Look, let me conjure it up for you."

A vast spectacle opens before Nachiketa's eyes; a celestial beauty contest is about to begin. If you have seen ancient Indian sculptures of the voluptuous heavenly damsels called *apsaras*, you will have some idea of what Nachiketa will see. An apsara's beauty is ageless, and it is not usually kept hidden either. Sanskrit poets say such a woman has eyes like wine; just to look at her makes you intoxicated. And now Yama, King of Death, brings out a vast parade of apsaras, each more breathtaking than the last. Miss Netherworld – Queen of the Land of Death. And here is Yama pointing out to Nachiketa the attractions of each candidate as she passes the reviewing stand in her chariot. "Just look at that one, Nachiketa! Doesn't your head swim to look at her? Look at that hair, like monsoon clouds. And you don't just get her, you get her chariot too!

"Besides," he confides, "they're all very gifted, you know. Schooled to perfection in the fine arts. They sing, they dance, they play the *vina*. You won't have to just sit and stare at each other."

Then he adds in a quiet whisper, "You just don't see girls like this on earth. There it's all done with a lot of makeup and ornaments. This is natural – and these girls won't get old. Please yourself, Nachiketa; don't hesitate."

Under these circumstances, I imagine, any red-blooded young man would just blurt out, "I'll take any of them!" But Yama says coolly, "Never mind. You don't have to choose now; take them all. But let's drop all this obsessive talk about the secret of life and death."

These offers are not the products of a tropical imagination. When desires are unified and the will becomes nearly invincible, every human capacity is deepened. To desire something *is* to will it, and to will is to achieve. If a person who has attained this state wants to become a great artist, build a bigger pyramid, explain the movements of the planets, he devotes his life to that, and usually he succeeds. So when Yama tells Nachiketa he can have whatever he wants – wealth, pleasure, power, fame – there is no need to refer to magic to understand that the offer is very real indeed. These are tests that every spiritual voyager has to face when he nears the end of his journey, only they do not usually come all together. They are spread out over a period of years, as we grow in our capacity to pass them. And Yama, hiding his impatience, waits for this sixteen-year-old to answer.

The reply would win the heart of any spiritual teacher. "Those are no blessings," the boy begins. "You're offering me a curse. I may be young, but I've got eyes. Don't you think I've seen people who have spent their lives running after pleasure or power? Their eyes are dull, their bodies weigh on them like lead; they can't find satisfaction anywhere. Even if I could live a thousand years, wouldn't I still end up like that?"

Death is silent; he cannot deny it. When prana goes, it *goes,* though it may take a thousand years.

"And what do you think, Mister Death? Can you make sense pleasures last forever?"

More silence. Even if the first piece of pie tastes indescribably delicious, nothing in the world can keep the fifth piece from being a bore.

"And after everything," the boy continues quietly, "after five hundred years, a thousand years, won't you still come and cut my life like a thread? What would all those pleasures amount to then, O Death? While I remain mortal, my life is not my own. As long as you allow me to live, I live; when you say 'come,' I go. What kind of life is that, dependent on your mercy?"

Nachiketa's voice rises now, almost as if he has lost his temper. "Who do you think I am, that you can buy me off with trinkets? You're not talking to an ordinary teenager, willing to give everything for skiing or sky-diving. Take your longevity, your elephants, your gold, your dancing girls and their chariots too. Keep them for yourself – and then come and tell me how long they satisfy you!"

Imagine entering the University of California as a freshman and saying, "Keep your bonehead English; here's my dissertation. Let me sit down and take my orals now." That is just what Nachiketa has done. If Death came and offered us what he has offered Nachiketa, even the most dedicated would be liable to ask for a year or two to sample before we choose. But Nachiketa doesn't hesitate. "Keep it for yourself!"

And nothing could please Death more. He looks the boy up and down and his face breaks into a smile. "Nachiketa," he says, "you would be a credit to any teacher. May I have more students like you!" Sure now that the boy will never waver, he begins to grant the third and final boon.

Chapter Two

Two Paths

IN SCHOOLS in village India, the first day of classes is different from all the rest. The headmaster gives a speech about the glory of the school, the glory of the teachers, the glory of the students; it is a very festive occasion. Only on the second day does the real work begin.

"Nachiketa," says Yama, "the first day is over. We've had our speeches; now let's get down to business – who you really are.

"Five layers of consciousness cover the Self, Nachiketa. Each must be reached through meditation, but meditation by itself is not enough. Every level brings new insights, which must be translated into daily behavior before you can progress to a deeper level. Merely to make this journey through consciousness means that personality is transformed.

"The outermost layer is the physical, the level of body-consciousness. Below this lie three layers which make up a kind of mental body – senses, emotions, and intellect. And nearest to the

Self is the ego, the individual sense of 'I.' Few can penetrate to this level, let alone go beyond it. Yet in every age, a handful do manage to discover they are neither body, mind, nor ego but the Self, who lives in the body and mind as their real operator.

"You will have to make this discovery yourself, Nachiketa; I cannot do it for you. But I will give you full instructions, and I will always be with you as your guide. With my blessings, you shall reach your goal."

Nachiketa is ready. "There is nothing else that I want, O Death, and I can have no better teacher than you. I am your devoted disciple; give me instruction."

Pleased, the King of Death begins. "Nachiketa," he says, "as a human being, you have been born with the capacity to make choices. No other creature has this capacity, and no human being can avoid this responsibility. Every moment, whether you see it or not, you have a choice of two alternatives in what you do, say, and think."

These alternatives have precise Sanskrit names that have no English equivalent: *preya* and *shreya*. Preya is what is pleasant; shreya, what is beneficial. Preya is that which pleases us, that which tickles the ego. Shreya, on the other hand, has no reference to pleasing or displeasing. It simply means what benefits us – that which improves our health or contributes to our peace of mind.

Preya, says the King of Death, pleases us *now*. It promises immediate gratification, and usually it delivers what it promises. The problem is that pleasure cannot last. All too soon it is past, and dissatisfaction sets in again. Preya just shrugs. "I'm a *now* man," he says. "I'm not responsible for the future; I live for today."

Shreya, on the other hand, is often unpleasant at the beginning, as anyone who has begun a physical fitness program knows. When you do your first sit-up after a decade of indolence, every muscle in the body goes out on strike. Only after a few weeks, if you stay with those exercises, do you begin to appreciate how much better you feel.

Most of us are used to door-to-door salesmen, trying to interest us in brushes or encyclopedias or biodegradable soaps. Preya and Shreya are no less dedicated salespeople. If you hide in the house and put up a sign saying "No Solicitors," they will barge right in. If you leave town and retire to a cave in the Adirondacks, they will come and seek you out. Sometimes – all too rarely – both are selling the same wares. Sometimes what is of lasting benefit is also very pleasant. But for the most part, Preya and Shreya are in direct competition.

Preya is a very sharp dresser. You could drop him into a singles bar and he would fit right in. With his bright-colored pants and plunging collar, a big Turkish mustache, and an outsized piece of exotic jewelry around his neck, Mr. Preya is an advertiser's dream. The moment you catch sight of him, you can't take your eyes away.

Shreya, on the other hand, looks a little mousy. Her features may be attractive, even pretty, but she is so unassuming that if she is standing right in front of us we usually do not notice. Two minutes after we are introduced to her we forget we have even met. When she tries to persuade us, she uses words we don't understand. In a word, as soon as we see Shreya, our attention wanders away.

But there is no doubt about Preya. He is an excellent salesman, and he knows exactly what he has to offer and who wants it. He makes his appeal directly to the senses or the ego. "Here's a good, dry beer," he tells the palate. In the background his competitor is objecting, "Ask him what a 'dry' beer is, for heaven's sake." But the palate is not interested in semantics. It only knows what it likes.

In a sense, both Preya and Shreya are promising the same thing: satisfaction. One you get immediately, but it comes and goes; the other requires effort, but its benefits stay with you.

Shreya, for example, does not tell us not to enjoy eating. She only points out that to make eating the purpose of life is contrary to good health. No one would deny that sugar tastes good. Everybody likes the taste of it, even a little microbe. If it were good for us too, as a four-year-old friend of mine says, we could eat it every day for breakfast, lunch, and dinner. "Why not?" says Preya. "If it feels good, do it."

Or take exercise. Not even Shreya would deny that there is a certain satisfaction in just sitting. Once you get used to it, the mere thought of movement becomes unpleasant. If your doctor suggests "moderate exercise," your skin begins to crawl.

"Why bother?" Preya whispers. "What does it matter? You're not going out for the Olympics. Your level of physical fitness is just right for your particular life-style." Unfortunately, your arteries are likely to feel the very same way. "Shut it down!" Even the blood starts to flow more slowly. Finally it will strain your heart simply to climb a flight of stairs. "You're courting a heart attack," says Shreya. "Get started on a fitness program before it's too late!"

Preya has a well-developed sales pitch for almost any product. He carries a little briefcase of graphs, tables, and other convincing multimedia presentations to bolster all his arguments. "The evidence is insubstantial," he says, pointing to his charts. "There is no controlled study to show that lung cancer or emphysema is caused by smoking. If the mortality rate for these diseases is higher among those who smoke, so what? Most of those people probably would have died even if they didn't smoke." "Sugar is just like any other carbohydrate – a great source of energy. Would you say energy is bad? Brush your teeth afterwards and you won't have anything to worry about."

In fact, Preya can be quite daring. He is not afraid of the Surgeon General; he flaunts that august gentleman's warnings on every box of cigarettes he sells. If the law requires him to print "Caution" in letters two feet high on every billboard, he will print them *three* feet high. Nothing can shake his self-confidence – and not without reason. He knows what he can sell. "Sure," he agrees, "the docs say they may kill you. Sure, if you're pregnant they may stunt the size and intelligence of your child. Let's be realistic: do you have a choice? Don't you *have* to do what you like? Come on, try 'em. You'll like 'em!"

Against all this, Shreya has a difficult time. Preya comes to our door with his bright smile and a big button on his lapel saying, "Alive with pleasure! Come to where the flavor is!" Who can hear

33

mild-mannered Miss Shreya, standing behind and saying quietly, "Turn the button over and see what it says: 'Come to where the cancer is. Alive with pleasure, dying in pain'"?

In fact, we don't want to hear Shreya. We think she wants to keep us from the things that make life enjoyable. Her wares are not unattractive at the outset – good health, security, peace of mind. We *would* like to have them, but they are not fun to have; it is painful to think of giving something up to gain them. Only when we lack these things do we realize that without them, life is unhappy indeed.

The Chariot and Its Rider

Nachiketa shakes his head. "There has to be more to the story. Even when we understand these choices, we often choose a direction that takes us where we don't really want to go."

Yama is pleased. "Exactly! Shreya and preya are roads that run in opposite directions, great highways that carry all human traffic. Every moment, Nachiketa, is a fork in life where two roads lead away before you. The first leads to the light of wisdom; the second, into darkness. Preya looks promising at the beginning, but no one likes its destination. Shreya seems uninviting, but it takes us where we want to go."

Let us look at the vehicles that travel these roads. Anyone who remembers *Ben-Hur* knows the kind of chariots they had in the ancient world. "Nachiketa," says Yama, "that is *you*. Your body is the chariot, drawn by five powerful horses, the senses. These horses travel not so much through space as time. They gallop, let us say, from birth towards death, pursuing the objects of their desire. The discriminating intellect – judgment – is the driver, whose job it is to see clearly and not drive you over a cliff. His reins are the mind, your emotions and desires. And you, Nachiketa, are the rider – the Self."

It is an image packed with implications. For one, there is a purpose to the mind. There is a reason why we have an intellect. The job of the intellect is to see clearly, and the job of the mind is to act as reins. When everything is working in harmony, we – the Self – make all the decisions. The intellect conveys these decisions to the mind – that is, to our desires – and all the senses obey the mind. But when the senses are uncontrolled, they immediately take to the road they like best: personal satisfactions, mostly pleasure. Then we are not making the decisions; the horses are.

To judge by what the media tell us, this is just the way things should be. Not only have most of us dropped the reins, our sense-horses have never even had a bit in their mouths. Instead of being trained, they have always been encouraged to do whatever they like. Should we wonder that they are wild? What *is* surprising is the power they have. I have seen a tiny palate, just a lot of microscopic taste buds, gallop into a bakery dragging a mountain of a man helplessly behind.

On the other hand, once these powerful horses are trained, they are as responsive as show horses. Imagine having strong, sensitive senses with a clear, discriminating intellect holding the reins. If the taste buds start to drag you away, you just give a tug on the will and all the senses understand. This is expert driving, and perfect living too. When the senses are trained, you can go anywhere and never lose your capacity to choose.

But there is much more to the chariot image than this. When someone asks how tall we are, don't we all respond with something like "Five foot seven"? If we have to describe ourselves we say, "I have blue eyes, brown hair, and a mole on my right cheek." Yama says, "Nonsense! Your *chariot* is five foot seven. Your chariot has blue eyes, brown hair, and a mole. You are not your chariot."

And what about the other statements we use so often? "I'm in a hurry." "I'm in a bad mood today." "I enjoy eating chocolate eclairs." Yama would retort, "You're still talking about your vehicle. Your chariot is in a hurry, your chauffeur overreacts, your horses love eclairs. All this 'I, I, I' is just confusion. You think you are the chariot and horses, that is all. You have forgotten who you really are, and all you can think about is, 'Is my feedbag full?' Your horses are happy when they get their éclair, so you think you are happy. They feel depressed when they can't get one, so you think you are depressed."

In a daring mood, he goes even further. "Just imagine: you *can't* be depressed. You can't really be insecure. Why? Because depression takes place in the mind; it is part of the chariot. You are the person who is paying for the trip – the one who stands in back and tells the driver where to go."

But there is a rub. When our horses want something not particularly beneficial – say, a martini – which of us can exercise our authority and say, "How about some lemonade instead?" The horses will smile to themselves and drop us off at the Happy Hour anyway. "I've got an alcohol problem," we explain. "Not at all," Yama would reply. "Your horses have an alcohol problem. You have a horse problem. You'd better get them trained."

Some years ago, to celebrate his birthday, I rashly took a young friend to a double bill of John Wayne Westerns. I had never seen a Western before, and I thought I was seeing the same film twice. Each, for example, had a long scene with a runaway stagecoach. "Sure," said my friend, who had obviously seen a lot of Westerns. "They *all* have a scene with a runaway stagecoach." And each had a lovely lady sitting inside, terrified out of her wits because her driver had been, shall we say, rendered incapable of further service by a band of robbers, and the horses were dragging the stage wherever they liked.

That, says Yama, is how most of us go through life. Our five horses are in the best of condition, full of spirit. In fact, we even give them pep pills from the media to keep them stirred up and restless. Unfortunately, however, nobody is holding the reins. The intellect is taking a nap at the driver's seat, and the horses drag us at a breakneck pace wherever they like, wherever a little money is waiting to be made or something exciting is going on. Inside – pure, unsullied, sequestered out of sight – is the lovely lady from Philadelphia, our real Self. If she could rouse the driver so that he could get hold of the reins and bring those horses under control, she would have an enjoyable ride. But as long as the horses are going where they like, the Self keeps the curtains drawn and simply prays for better days.

Doesn't this agree with the experience of most of us? Here, let us say, it is time for lunch, so the Self opens her curtain ever so slightly. "Driver," she calls out in her still, small voice, "it is time to eat. Please take my carriage to Old Healthy's Café, where we can get whole-grain bread and some homemade soup."

"Right, lady," the intellect says. He is willing enough, and he is quite polite. But he has been tipping the elbow since breakfast; his eyes can't see clearly and his judgment feels fuzzy.

The coach takes off in a cloud of dust. After a while the Self gets apprehensive and takes a peek through her window. "Driver, driver! This is not the way to Old Healthy's! Where are you taking me?"

"Relax, lady," the intellect says. His speech is a little blurred. "Fact is, I sort of dropped the reins soon as we turned the corner."

Of course, the senses go straight where they always go – Giovanni's. Only after we have finished our beer and pizza do we remember we were on a diet. "I really *do* want to lose weight," we say. "Why did I go and do that?"

Nachiketa must be nodding as he hears all this. Now he can see why life as it is ordinarily lived seems so backwards. We all want happiness, security, love, the satisfaction of a life worth living. Why do we go in the other direction? Because nobody has the reins.

The Road to Wisdom

When we let the senses follow their own lead, they cannot help going after pleasure; that is their nature. As a result, it should come as no surprise to see that most of the world today is on the road to sensory satisfaction. Shreya scarcely sees a horse. Everybody is galloping towards Preya, whose road looks like Churchill Downs in the middle of the Kentucky Derby.

Look at our popular magazines, especially the advertisements; go where the greatest numbers of people go when they have leisure.

Pleasure is another kind of perennial philosophy, an age-old, virtually universal faith.

In this light, I think we show a very pious nature. Most Americans, for example, close their evenings with several hours of prayer. There is an altar in the living room of virtually every home in this country. As soon as the light is lit an awe comes over us, an almost hypnotic readiness to believe. Then the high priest comes onto the screen and tries to sell us things.

In the Middle Ages, when the Catholic Church fell on hard times for a while, it used to sell indulgences that were supposed to atone for sins. These priests of the media sell us vacuum cleaners, automobiles, toothpaste, deodorant, and all sorts of things much more harmful than indulgences ever were. The background music, the unctuous tones of affected interest, soothe us and beguile our trust. These are people who care. They are so concerned about our welfare that they will take any hour of the day or night to attract our attention if we do not have this particular kind of toothpaste or travel in that kind of car.

And look at the arguments: "Indulge yourself." "Live a little!" "Don't you deserve the best?" The underlying message is all the same: *Pleasure is everything*. Wherever pleasure is promised you will find people flocking in, putting down their money, their vitality, and their time, and saying, "*This* is living!"

The other day I saw an advertisement that began, "The great restaurants of Europe in ten food-filled days!" That is a pilgrimage, Nachiketa would say, as arduous as walking from Lourdes to Jerusalem. You go from shrine to shrine paying homage, and when it is all over you carry home some sacred relics: an eight-page menu, a napkin stamped "Fedulucci's of Firenze," a wine bottle from Le Coq d'Or.

In Bede's history of England, the Anglo-Saxon king Edwin is approached by emissaries from Rome to persuade him to embrace the Christian faith. Edwin consults his two most trusted advisors, one of whom is a rather pragmatic man. "Sire," he says, "I have worshipped the old gods most of my life, yet I do not have what I want. Can this new religion offer me fulfillment? If it can, I will embrace it, for the way I have followed has not taken me where I want to go."

Where has the religion of pleasure taken us? I doubt that there has ever been a time in history when it was followed with greater fervor. Yet there has never been a time when human beings felt more alienated, more desolate, more cut off from those around them.

The reply of Edwin's other counselor will probably be remembered as long as English is read. "It has often seemed to me that our life on earth is like a swallow that suddenly darts into a brightly lit banquet hall on a stormy night, lingers a moment, and then darts out a window at the other side. It comes from the wintry darkness into the warmth and light, and for a moment we see it clearly. Then it disappears again into the darkness outside.

"That is how my life appears to me. I do not know from where I came into this world or where I am going; all I know is a brief span of light which I fly through all too swiftly. If your new religion can tell me why I am here and what lies before and after me, then I for one will follow it with all my heart."

This is not presented as a moral issue. Death is not a moralist. He simply shrugs and says, "You can choose." In the end, the problem with preya is simply that it runs away from shreya: that is, away from health, security, and peace of mind.

When my wife and I were in one of the big cities of India many years ago, we had to go from our hotel to a bank where I had never been before. After some looking, we managed to find a taxi driver who cordially agreed to take us. It was a very picturesque trip. We saw a good deal of the city, and we paid well for the experience too. Only later did I discover that the man had taken us all around the city before letting us off a few blocks from where we had been.

That is what Yama is trying to convey: we go through life like this. We may enjoy the scenery, but only rarely does someone like Nachiketa object, "Hey, look at the meter! You've been driving me around this way for twenty years. Let's take a different route."

The real issue here is choice. If you had a car that could turn only one way, would you say that it is free? If it ran around crashing into things because it could not turn, denting its fenders and wasting all its fuel, would you shrug and say, "That's automotive nature. That's my car's mode of self-expression"? It would take you a long time to get anywhere, and where you arrived would not be up to you.

"Everybody likes a responsive car," Yama says. "Wouldn't you like to have a responsive mind?"

The other day I set out for a drive through the California wine country. With a car that did not obey me, as far as I could tell, I might have ended up about a hundred miles away at the River's End restaurant, where the Russian River empties into the sea.

It is tragic, but many lives are like that. "People *do* want to learn to live," Yama explains to Nachiketa. "But they just don't know how to steer their cars. Sixty, seventy, eighty years later, after a lot of stops and right-turn detours, they are out of gas at River's End. Then there is nothing to do but go inside, get something to drink, and recall a line or two from Swinburne: 'Even the weariest river winds somewhere safe to sea.' There is no sense of fulfillment in life then, only a hollow feeling that something essential has been missed. The auto club has to come and say compassionately, 'You're not going to get any further with that old car. The steering's rigid; the column is frozen tight. Better come back with another vehicle and try again.'"

Nachiketa nods grimly. Young though he is, he seems to know that feeling. He does not want to experience it again.

"I understand," he tells Yama simply. "Now tell me how to choose. How do I take the road that leads to wisdom?"

"Very simple," the King of Death replies with his fearful smile. "Just don't take the other road."

That is all. When we do not choose preya, we are choosing shreya. It is a most encouraging truism. Sri Ramakrishna, with the simplicity of a child, used to give the same advice: "If you want to go east, don't go west."

Simple to say, but terribly difficult to do. "You have to be tough," Yama tells his young pupil. "Really tough. Can you grasp the reins from under those flying hooves and rein your horses in? Can you train them to go where you decide? It can't be done in a few weeks. The greatest of men and women have taken years to train their senses and passions."

When Preya comes and gives his sales pitch, the person with little endurance immediately says, "Wrap them up. I'll take a dozen." It takes real toughness to wait out all the blandishments of passing pleasures when they lead us away from our real goal. Teresa of Avila called it *determinación:* resoluteness, resolve, the capacity to go on trying and never give up.

When we lack this toughness, despite better goals we may cherish in our hearts, we will not be able to take the road that leads where we want to go. It is a poignant paradox: wanting only happiness, yet going systematically in the other direction. But if we keep on choosing shreya, Yama assures us, we *will* reach our goal.

Fortunately for all of us, we need not be born with this kind of inner toughness. Very few human beings are. This is a quality that ᵗe learned, as systematically as we learn to play the piano, and ᵗng of Death is about to show us how.

ᴺachiketa, the myth concludes, learned from the King of Death the full secret of life and death. With this knowledge he returns to the world of mortals, no longer sixteen years old but eternal, sure of life's purpose and overflowing with the desire to pass his knowledge on to others. As long as men and women seek to overcome death, his story will be told: not only to inspire, but to show how to follow this daring teenager's journey into consciousness and make his discovery for ourselves.

Chapter Three

The City of Eleven Gates

THE JOURNEY into consciousness begins at the physical level, the level of the body. Most of us take it for granted that this is what we are. "I am my body; when my body dies, I die." How we came to believe this superstition is a great mystery, the most grievous case of mistaken identity I can imagine.

To show the consequences of this belief, Yama brings in another wonderfully compact image. In India, many cities have poetic names ending in *pur* or *pura,* which simply means "city." There is Udaipur, the City of Dawn, Nagpur, the City of Elephants, and Jaipur, the City of Victory, once described by an English traveler as "a rose-red city half as old as time." Even Singapore takes its name from Sanskrit: *Simha-pura,* the City of Lions. In the same poetic spirit, Yama calls the human body *Ekadasha-dvara-pura,* the City of Eleven Gates.

To see how apt an image this is, we have only to look at the cities of the ancient world. Whether we are talking about Old Testament Jerusalem, York in the Middle Ages, or Ur of the Chaldees six thousand years ago, it is interesting how similar they were in the essentials. Most prominently, there was almost always a wall to provide protection. The most vital places in these walls were the gates, above which huge towers usually rose on left and right. Inside, the chronicles tell us, even the most ancient cities were full of intense activity. As many people as could live within the walls did so, and most of those who were left outside the city came there regularly to trade. And often, on a high, secluded place, there was a great citadel where the ruler of the city lived, surrounded by beautiful gardens or courtyards, with an imposing view of the world around.

This is a good description of the human body too. The skin, of course, is the wall. In terms of evolution, it must have developed for much the same reasons, to provide protection and define structures for proper functioning. The street map is Gray's *Anatomy*. And no city ever throbbed with more activity. To a microbe, the body must be a world much like medieval Amsterdam with its canals: red blood cells running around delivering nutrients and collecting garbage, tissues constantly being repaired, neurons humming with interoffice memos. Even our bones, I am told, are in a continuous state of urban renewal. It is a highly complex scenario – yet, as we shall see, only a small part of the whole picture of who we are.

The eleven gates to this bustling city are the bodily openings. Seven are in the head: two side doors, two big bay windows in front, below them two small flues for smelling things, and below that one huge barn door. Then there are the organs of reproduction and evacuation, which makes nine. But the last two gates are harder to guess. One is the navel; the other probably corresponds to the sagittal suture, the tiny fissure that divides the bones of the skull at the very crown of the head.

The significance of these last two gateways is marvelous. Through the first we take in life, the sustenance of the mother, until birth. At that moment the tenth gate closes, never to open again. And the eleventh gate is only opened when the man or woman who

43

has achieved Self-realization sheds the body. According to the long mystical tradition of Hinduism, those who gain complete control over consciousness are able to gather all their prana together when death is imminent and slip out the eleventh gate like a spiritual Houdini – allowing the body to die, as it were, by an act of will. This secret escape-way has been provided for all of us to use, but only one in a million knows what it is for and how to find it.

If the body is a city, who or what are we? The answer is that we are the ruler, the king or queen. We have a citadel in the very center of the city – the citadel of the mind, in which there are many wonderful chambers. And in the innermost recesses of this citadel are the royal chambers where the ruler dwells – the Self. That is our real home. We are free to roam around, but we should always be able to return to these innermost chambers for strength and rest.

Unfortunately, however, all this has been forgotten. Like the young prince in Mark Twain's story, we have left home to lead the life of a pauper out by the city walls; but instead of remembering that it is just a game, we have been gone so long that we have forgotten we were ever ruler at all. Instead we pass our lives on sentry duty, going from one sense-gate to the next. "Watchman, what of the watch? Anything to see? Anything to hear?" A nice-looking sense object passes by and the eyes call out, "Hey, let *that* in!" Along comes a familiar tune and the ears say, "Open us up too!" And when something good to eat appears on the horizon – say, a chocolate éclair – eyes, mouth, and nostrils all open wide, and that one éclair goes in five doors at once.

Unfortunately, these sense-impressions are not merely visitors. They come in to stay. Most of us do not have immigration quotas or ask for identification at the gates; we let everybody in. After a while there is a housing problem; the mind is full of vagabonds. There is an employment problem, because so many idle impressions are running about with nothing constructive to do. They even get into the castle, where they make themselves at home. "Oh, the king's gone, is he? Well, that's all right. We'll wait." They eat up everything in the house, throw their clothes around, put on the royal robes, sleep in the king-size bed. And no one is in City Hall. *We* are the ruler, but we are out on the battlements, helping to open the gates to let more intruders in.

All in all, it is a busy, all-absorbing life. By the end of the day we are tired. If, as we drop off to sleep, we happen to hear a little voice inquiring, "Say, how are things going in the castle?" we simply mutter, "What castle?"

Senses and Vitality

In all this hubbub we not only forget we are rulers of our city, we begin to identify ourselves with the walls and gates. If Queen Elizabeth began signing her checks "London Bridge," we would find it absurd; yet we do much the same thing countless times every day. If the senses are attracted to something, we think *we* are attracted. If we hear about a new sensation, most of us have to sample it.

When we cannot control our eating, for example, we are identifying ourselves with the gate of taste. When something appetizing approaches, we have no choice but to open ourselves wide and desire it. "Bring it through! Always room for something more."

I was amazed to read the other day that there are people who eat twenty-five times a day. Where does it all go? How can it even be processed? After all, it takes about four hours for a meal to be digested. For four hours there is a little sign on the City Manager's door: "Do not disturb! Business in progress." If you drop by a friend's house an hour after breakfast and sit down for a couple of brownies, you are barging into the office and announcing, "Break it up, boys! I've got some new agenda."

Big and Little Intestine will object, "The old agenda are still on the table."

"Never mind," you say. "Let it wait. These brownies are non-negotiable."

The consequences of this are much more than physical. What is lost first is choice. Medieval cities, to illustrate, had gates to keep people out as much as to let them through. You had to state your business, show your credentials, and pay your gate tax before you could get in. Without such control the city would have been in chaos, even in times of peace. Similarly, sense-impressions should not barge in; they should wait politely while we examine their credentials. If they are beneficial, or at least harmless, we can allow them into our consciousness. But if they are a selfish crew who will come and eat up a lot of prana, a lot of our vitality, we should have no hesitation about telling them, "Stay out!"

Take another set of gates, the eyes. Even when we are innocently window-shopping, an unmistakable look comes into the eyes. Our consciousness is up front at those two gates, and with a little imagination you can see them opening to gobble up everything they see. Some gift stores have a little sign: "If you break it, you've bought it." Yama would say, "If you gobble it, you've bought it" – even if you only gobble with your eyes. You have paid for it with something much more precious than money; a part of your vitality has gone out.

This may sound occult, but test it. Go to a store full of things you would like to have and take a few hours walking around, just looking. When you go home, how do you feel? Most of us are drained after a morning of window-shopping, and not because we have been on our feet. At every counter, even if we haven't bought anything, an unseen clerk has rung up her prana register. "You don't need to carry any cash," she says. "Just give me your Master Charge." We may not feel our wallets get lighter, but just as with a credit card, the bill *does* come due.

The gates of the senses open only one way: outward. Prana can only go out through the senses; it cannot come in. And what opens the gates is desire. The mind gets excited, and the fierce craving to see, to taste, to touch, to hear, to smell, rushes to the appropriate sense-gates and throws them open. Prana gushes out, and there is temporary enjoyment – until the supply of prana is drained.

While prana is pouring out, it is very difficult to pull the senses closed again. But when the outflow finally subsides, nothing remains to keep the senses open. A kind of vacuum has been created inside. The doors bang shut, and we are sealed in.

This is depression. The greater the degree of excitement, the deeper the reaction that sets in: perhaps a six-week bout, perhaps only a subclinical "low." In any case, it is a kind of solitary confinement; the mind has nothing to do but brood upon itself. The things that formerly seemed exciting now elicit no response, because there is no prana with which to respond. The senses are closed. You can talk to that person and he will not hear; you can take him to a movie and he may not even follow the plot. He is utterly absorbed in a Hall of Mirrors inside, in which he and everyone else are pushed, pulled, and twisted into fantastic shapes. One side of him looks huge, the rest is shrunken. A friend's smile becomes a grimace; a look becomes a leer. If this goes on long enough, a depressed person can come to believe that these distortions are real.

More than that, as can happen in solitary confinement, time seems to stop. You think you have always been in this state and always will be; you cannot remember that every depression comes to an end. The results can be tragic: as we know, it is all too common for severe depression to end in suicide.

To relate to other people, to function in the world, consciousness has to be able to flow out; that is why the sense windows open outwards. But the mind is not made to stand open all the time. It is not able to stay in a state of constant stimulation, to withstand a state of continuous excitement. In this sense, depression is a kind of safety mechanism. When you try to plug too many appliances into one circuit, as everyone knows, you blow a fuse. It is irritating, but much better than burning up the wires with too much current. Depression is similar: it shuts down the senses and allows time for the prana tank to fill again.

The biochemical approach to depression is to force the windows open again with a powerful drug. In extreme cases this may be necessary as first aid, but because the will is not involved, the depression is all too likely to recur. There are, however, a number of effective ways of treating depression where it starts: within the mind.

For first aid, the goal is to get the windows open. This is terribly difficult, for you have to go against the conditioning of your situation. In a word, you have to do everything that your mind is crying out *not* to do: be with other people, work with them, make yourself take an active interest in what they are doing and saying. You may feel bilious, but make yourself smile. And be physically active; throw yourself into hard, productive, physical work. All these things turn attention away from yourself by directing it outward. You are drawing directly on the will, which pours prana back into the tank. And as the tank fills, the senses and mind revive and the sense-windows open. Once that happens the depression is gone; you are alive again.

That is first aid, but even more important are the preventive measures. Depression is an energy crisis; we can avoid the crisis by conserving gas. In other words, the time to guard against depression is when we are getting excited, by not overindulging the senses or the mind. Overeating wastes prana, essentially through the desire to eat. Similarly with other wild movements in the mind: anger, resentment, worry, vacillation.

Wherever there is excitement, depression has to follow, as certainly as sitting in a parked car with your foot on the accelerator has to burn up gas. The car does not need to be going anywhere, and similarly we do not have to be doing anything. We can burn a whole tankful of prana simply in the mind. Dwelling on ourselves, magnifying personal problems, replaying the past, worrying about the future, inflating desires, withdrawing into a private never-never land of fantasies, all waste incredible amounts of prana.

That is one reason why I speak out against the excessive emphasis our civilization places on sex − especially sex as a sensation, for gratification alone. Sex has a beautiful place in a completely loyal, loving relationship, where it expresses with great tenderness a desire for union on more than simply a physical level. But dwelling on sex wastes prana the way an RV does gas. It is no coincidence that today, when the emphasis on sex has never been greater, depression is almost epidemic.

I have a teenage friend with an elaborate sound system in his room, where he can sit with his earphones on and listen to music as loud as he likes. You can call his name, pound on his door, do whatever you like; he will not hear. The expression on his face will tell you that he is not even in this world; he is off in a little realm all his own.

Many people today tune in like this to their own minds. They hide away in some corner, put earphones over their ears, and listen in complete absorption to their own thoughts. If the combination of hi-fi and earphones is insidious, the "in-fi" is much more so, for it cuts us off from others around us. We don't hear them, don't really even see them; we lose all sensitivity to their needs.

A Colossal Fallacy

After some time of all this confusion, we come to believe that there is nothing else to the city except its walls and gates. If we admit to the existence of a citadel – the mind – all we will talk about is its physical facade. In other words, we think we are purely physical entities, biochemical organisms that can be satisfied by biochemical means. It is a colossal fallacy, one that has cost the modern world its health and its peace.

'en it comes to health, for example, most of us – and most of dical world – think in terms of walls. We like to keep the ainted, hang up shields, and decorate the gates with ban-
d when someone asks, "How are you today?" we reply,
uldn't be better! Just look at my walls." Inside the citadel of the mind, unfortunately, it is often a different story. The foundation may be crumbling, the chambers are dark, the courtiers may even be plotting revolution. Only by learning to meditate can we actually get inside the mind and begin to clean things up. Then it is that we really start to *enjoy* good health – spiritual, mental, and physical. It is a subtle point, but a wall cannot enjoy being well built. Only the ruler knows the satisfaction of living in a clean, harmonious place.

On the other hand, when we live in a world of appearances, we think appearance is the whole of living. If Juliet has certain physical proportions, silky hair, clear skin, and thirty-two clean, white teeth, we say, "What a beautiful woman!" Even without taking a spiritual perspective, it is a very limited notion of beauty. We have stopped thinking about the ruler inside. The citadel may be abandoned and full of bats; it does not matter. If the battlements are well-built and colorful banners flutter above the gates, we say, "What a handsome king! What a lovely queen!"

If this sounds exaggerated, look at any popular fashion magazine and see how we equate appearance with personality. Admittedly fashion is a world that most people agree is unreal. But on the other hand, many fashion designers seem quite successful, from which I infer that somebody must believe in them. These men and women are contemporary prophets. We shape our lives around their words and wares, which go much deeper than cosmetics. When somebody persuades you to change the shape of your mouth each season, or tells you that you can't be seen in society this year unless your clothes don't fit in a particular way, he is telling you that these things make up your personality. If that is what personality is, it is no wonder that so many people feel insecure about who they really are.

Here I think nothing goes so far as plastic surgery. "The choice is coming!" one magazine proclaims. "Do you want a new car this year, or a new face?" We don't simply identify with the body any more; we think we are the top five millimeters of our skin. For someone used to seeing the person underneath, the effect of plastic surgery is quite disquieting: to me, an older person without the lines of age is like a clock without hands. We may buy some time, but when the wrinkles come back again, we are going to be more insecure than ever. Ironically, when we identify ourselves with the body, wrinkles come back faster than ever; crows come and dance under our eyes.

From my perspective, manipulating our appearance like this is ungrateful at best. The body is an owner-built home, shaped by what we think, say, and do. After we have designed our house, built it, painted it, and decorated it, the least we can do is make ourselves at home. If we want a change, we can change the way we think.

Imagine you are a girl in her teens, stunningly attractive, and you have finally managed a date with the boy of your dreams. He is due at seven, so you start getting ready at five-thirty; for an hour and a half you go on getting ready over and over again.

Finally you hear his car outside, and you rush to throw open the door. For a moment, your heart is in your mouth. What will he think? Will he like your dress? Will his pulse race when he smells the flowers in your hair?

Fortunately, he is stunned. "Wow!" He rushes up the stairs and reaches out his arms – but not for you. "What a house! Look at all that redwood! Is this a Greene and Greene?"

"Green *what*, silly? This is powder blue!"

"Nice burnt brick, too. And that leaded glass is great."

He goes on and on about the wood, the fixtures, the lighting, the plants, until finally he recollects himself and looks at his watch. "Hey, it's late! I'd better be going. Thanks for a great time."

If I know anything about teenagers, that fellow would earn a title I never heard in any English class in India: "creep." But this is how most of us behave, women and men, when we enter a relationship. Our attention is on the house; we scarcely notice the person who lives inside.

In a Marx brothers movie there is a scene in which Groucho is embracing, I think, Mae West. "Hold me closer," she pleads. "Honey," Groucho replies, "if I hold you any closer, I'll come out on the other side." That is a rather good observation. You can squeeze two houses together until the walls crumble, but as far as relationships go, the occupants will achieve better communication over the telephone.

Our whole way of life today is telling us that to have rich, rewarding relationships with the opposite sex, we should cultivate the company of houses and doors. It should not be surprising that many marriages now do not last longer than a few years, and casual relationships not longer than a few weeks. Often people become bitterly disappointed in such cases, not only with their partner but with themselves. But how can there be a relationship between two houses? The people involved are not even there. Two empty cottages are sitting side by side and saying, "We can't talk. We can't share. We're only houses; we don't know how to communicate."

"The Garden of Allah"

My wife has a weakness for old movies, so I once took her to a nineteen-thirties film called *The Garden of Allah*. The plot reminded me of Francis Thompson's image of God as the "Hound of Heaven," tracking us all down. Charles Boyer plays a young man in a monastery who begins to think about all the things he must be missing in the world outside. Finally he slips away, and when we see him next he is at the edge of the Sahara. Soon Marlene Dietrich appears, and for a while he tries to lose himself in the pleasures of a meaningful relationship in the "Garden of Allah" – the desert. Strolling in evening clothes across alluring sands, dining with cut glass and candlelight in colorful Bedouin tents, he seems to have everything he was looking for.

But the Hound of Heaven is hot on his trail. The more he struggles, the more he is torn by his deep desire to find something real and lasting. And finally, after much soul-searching, he goes back to his monastery; nothing the world offers is enough to satisfy him.

Yama, I think, would find this a good setting for a much vaster drama. Our City of Eleven Gates is much like those desert settlements, from whose sun-baked walls we scan the horizon for something to interest the senses. And somehow we find the view alluring. The sands shift constantly; the colors change; mirages beckon with the promise of lush oases. And after a while, not content with what the sense-world brings us, we decide to go outside.

The surprising thing is that there is nothing outside to attract us. Without exaggeration, sensory pleasure *is* a mirage. It may be exciting to pursue it, but every time we taste it, we come away thirstier than we were before. This is the illusion the Hindu mystics call *maya*. We thirst for satisfaction, and there are living waters in the citadel inside. But our eyes are turned outwards, we do not remember that there is a citadel, and out we go into the desert in search of shimmering promises that lead us farther and farther away.

Imagine spending your whole life in the desert – eating there, sleeping there, working there, playing there. You have a citadel with a king-size bed, but you prefer your sleeping bag. You have a palatial kitchen, but you have grown accustomed to your fire pit. And when the sun goes down and the temperature plummets, you huddle outdoors and shiver. If someone asks why you don't go inside, you reply, "What's 'inside'? I've lived this way all my life, and so have my parents and my grandparents too."

The vast majority of human beings live very much like this. Because they do not know how to enter the deeper levels of consciousness, they are exposed to all the storms that life can bring. When fortune smiles they get excited, when she frowns they get dispirited or depressed, all because the lifeline that connects them with the source of security and wisdom has been cut.

While we are close to the center of our being we are safe; when we are far from it, we are in peril. In the search for external satisfaction, we can wander so far from this citadel of safety that we lose sight of everything except the world of the senses, the world of physical appearance. And there we get into serious trouble.

In the early days of sensory exploration, most of us do not wander very far. But gradually the lines of communication become so long that supplies cannot reach us; vitality cannot be sent. We go half a day's journey away, then a whole day's journey; and that means we have to bivouac overnight, away from shelter. We put up a little tent on the sands or move into a cave, where we identify ourselves completely with our senses, and our connection with the center of consciousness is broken.

If you have never spent a night at the edge of the Sahara, I would advise you to avoid it. Shifting sands may look fascinating by day, but as soon as the sun disappears – and in the desert it disappears abruptly – the world puts on a very different face. Where it was hot, it suddenly becomes bitter cold. Where there was so much light that it hurt your eyes, there is suddenly no light at all. And all kinds of creatures that hide during the heat of the day come out at night to prowl. You can hear them, but usually you cannot see them; it is a highly unpleasant combination.

At night, in short, the lure of the desert vanishes. In place of fascination you feel lost, lonely, homesick, a little afraid. You want to get back, but you can no longer see. If you start to wander, you may completely lose track of where you are. The Bedouin have many stories about those whom the desert swallows; they do not usually return.

When this happens, you really are alone. Formerly you could at least go to the radio every now and then and talk to headquarters. You did not define yourself as an isolated entity; you still felt some sense of unity with family and friends. But once you get caught outside yourself, that vital connection is gone. Your friend Jane may still visit you; Jack may still come now and then to bring your mail. But it is harder and harder to find you, and it is a different person that they find. When they remind you about old friends, old haunts, you do not remember. You have even forgotten the safety of your castle, the spacious courtyards, the gardens. The desert is everything; the desert is all you know. After a while, most friends stop making that journey. All they find is a ghost town; there is nobody at home. If you want to see the tragic proof, look at the faces on the streets in any metropolitan area, especially after dark.

In the Sahara, I am told, it is still possible to come across the remains of a long-abandoned city, surrounded by thousands of square miles of empty desert. In Roman days it would have been part of a vital network connecting many other cities and towns. But the desert spread; the supply routes grew too difficult. Now such places are isolated and alone. Buildings crumble, sand drifts over the fallen stones, and after a while the snakes and scorpions think it has been their home since the beginning of time.

To clear out and restore such a city is a huge archaeological endeavor. I would only ask, why go so far? Each of us has his own city to restore, with an inner citadel much more difficult or dangerous to explore than Major Laing found Timbuktu. It takes a good deal of patient digging to realize the truth of what all the great religions tell us: this is not just any old city; it is nothing less than the city of God.

Once we get within the citadel — what Saint Teresa calls the "interior castle" — we find another world. Our eyes have become used to the "garish day" outside; until we get our bearings, we are likely to stumble a little. But gradually we see with surprise that the inside of the citadel is much vaster than what lies outside. Between the body and the Self are whole worlds to be traversed — the worlds of the mind.

Chapter Four

Gross and Subtle

BELOW THE SURFACE of consciousness, we begin to see that we have really been living not in one body but in two – one, as it were, right inside the other, as a lining within a glove.

In yoga psychology, the outermost of these two is called *sthula-sharira*, the "gross body." This is the physical organism, with which we are most familiar. But the gross body has a kind of double, made of energy just as the physical body is made of chemical elements. It is called *sukshma-sharira*, the "subtle body," and it corresponds roughly to what we call the mind – our feelings, desires, intellect, and will.

Gross Body is kindly enough, but no intellectual. He does not go in for ballet or read demanding literature; he likes straightforward physical activity and sensible, uncomplicated pleasures. And, it must be confessed, he usually pays little attention to his partner, Subtle.

Subtle, on the other hand, does her best to be sure that her grosser half meets her needs. Hers is a demanding and highly sensitive nature. And she is as ethereal as a Gothic heroine: she doesn't simply walk, she glides, so noiselessly that Gross scarcely knows she is around. One look at her eyes will tell you that she lives in a different world, an inner realm where time, cause, and effect are subject to her whim. Without exaggeration it is a dream world, for when we dream, only Gross is asleep. Awareness is withdrawn from the body and senses and consolidated in the subtle body, the domain of thoughts and feelings.

To philosophers, the relationship between Gross and Subtle poses serious problems. If the two are so different, how do they communicate? Either we have to explain how physical events in the body can be caused by something not physical – what professor Gilbert Ryle called the "ghost in the machine" theory of body and mind – or we have to explain one in terms of the other, which usually means reducing the mind to physics and chemistry.

The rest of us, of course, do not usually worry about such conundrums. All we know is that when we experience a strong emotion like anger, we *feel* the knots in our stomach. If we hear distressing news that touches us personally, we feel the body go into shock, just as it would if we had fallen down the stairs. After a day of criticism at work, we do not need a physiologist to tell us that our body has spent eight hours geared up for "fight or flight," despite the absence of any physical threat. And when a young man embraces his girlfriend, all kinds of things happen with body chemistry that do not happen when he embraces his Aunt Claire. We may not know how these things happen, but Subtle clearly does play a role in how Gross responds.

In the last decade or so, the discussion of mind-body relationships has been lifted out of philosophy into science, as researchers in medicine and psychology have turned to the study of how the mind – or, more precisely, "psychosocial factors" – might affect the body in health, illness, and healing.

Some of this research is brilliantly suggestive. There is good evidence that there is communication on a molecular level among the immune system, the central nervous system (particularly the brain), and the endocrine system, whose glands moderate how the body responds in various states of emotion. And there are intriguing studies which indicate that the immune system can be conditioned by the brain, and countless studies of possible connections between emotional states and illness. Today, says Dr. Robert Ader, a pioneer in the new field of psychoneuroimmunology, "the issue is not whether psychosocial factors influence disease. The question is how."

"How" probably includes millions of connections through which the mind is involved in health and illness. But one underlying influence goes unsuspected, though I doubt that any single factor has a greater impact: our deep, unquestioning belief that the physical body is what we are.

Most of us would not agree that we think this. We would probably maintain that we have an inner self of some sort, however vaguely understood. But that is not how we behave. To see what people really believe, look at what they actually do: what they work for, what goals they pursue, what they do to entertain themselves, how they spend their time and energy and money. Watch a few hours of television; check the current movies; look through the magazines at your local supermarket; listen to a selection of popular songs. Most significantly, look at the advertisements and commercials. We live in a sea of media conditioning that reflects back to us what we value, and the message we are saturated with is simple and axiomatic: "You are your body. The human being is a purely physical creature whose needs can be satisfied on the physical level." It is one of the most destructive superstitions I can imagine, with adverse effects throughout a society — not least of which is its effect on personal health.

"*I Am My Body*"

Gross Body, naturally, is highly physically oriented. If he cannot see, hear, smell, taste, or touch something, it simply does not exist. Consequently, his attention is all on the outward appearance of things. He may not hear what you are saying, but if one of your buttons does not match, he will notice and call your attention to it. If you comment on the Rolls Royce down the street, he will point out that it is really a Bentley. In the middle of a conversation his attention will be caught by a glimpse of someone behind you, and he will interrupt to point out irrelevantly, "Hey, that guy looks just like my Uncle Freddy!" And of course, his relationships with other people will be based on how they look.

There are many people like this today, and the things that capture their attention can really be surprising. I have known men whose measure of feminine beauty was the leg – or, stranger still, the knee. I can understand being captivated by a beautiful face, but by a knee? And as for legs, I like the remark of President Lincoln: "I am satisfied as long as they reach the ground."

One or two boys in my high school had this kind of obsession about hair. Women in Kerala pride themselves on long, rich, cascading black hair, which is often entwined with flowers. Each girl in our class had her favorite flowers and her special ways of wearing them, so that our schoolroom used to look and smell like a garden. Now, no one would deny that long, black hair entwined with jasmine makes an attractive setting for a lovely face. But I had one friend who was not particularly interested in looking at a face. When the rest of us boys would sit in front, this fellow would stay in the back where all he could see was hair. "Why not?" he would shrug. "I know what I like."

This may seem singular, but it is startling to realize that millions of people – not only men but women too, as we can see in the popular magazines – unconsciously make very similar equations about others, and even about themselves. Yet reducing people to part of the body is no more absurd than identifying ourselves with the body at all.

When a person's attention is caught in physical appearance like this, superficial differences are magnified. We get disturbed all out of proportion over little, little things, and judge people around us on the basis of physical characteristics – even clothes! – that have nothing to do with the individuals themselves. And the more we identify ourselves with our own body, the narrower our idea of what is acceptable.

Young people, to take just one example, are inclined to behave as if everyone over sixty belongs to another planet. When insecurity over age is acute, it becomes "Never trust anyone over thirty." Few of us examine the underlying logic: "I am my body, and my body looks young; therefore anybody whose body does *not* look young is a different kind of being. Their thinking processes must be different, their values must be different; why should I even listen to them?"

Of course, the very nature of the body is to be physically isolated. The more we identify ourselves with it, the more alienated we become. For many people, there comes a time when nobody qualifies for acceptance except their peer group, where everyone looks and talks and seems to feel the same.

This is scarcely a problem of young people alone. In striking contrast to the traditional societies of world history, where age is venerated, our modern industrial society worships youth – or, more accurately, a youthful appearance. Ironically, when a person with this perspective becomes a senior citizen, the gap of distrust remains – only then he or she is on the other side. "Never trust anyone *under* thirty!" The teenager who viewed aged pedestrians as road obstacles now drives a slow-moving RV with stickers that proclaim "I've paid my dues," lives in a retirement community that walls young people out, and contemplates legislation that would raise the voting age to thirty-five – ironically, while still doing his best to look and act as young as possible.

At its most extreme, this way of thinking threatens violence around the world. "I am my body; nobody who looks different has a right to live in my society." As I write this, South Africa is still being torn apart by racial war, and ethnic supremacist groups are systematically attacking and destroying minorities in every major continent on the planet – including, tragically, my own state of California.

Insecurity

Because of this hypersensitivity to external appearances, people who are highly body-conscious are characteristically insecure. Their moods and self-esteem are at the mercy of little changes around them, so their security can be shaken by a misinterpreted word, a glance, an unexpected turn of events, which they magnify and take personally. They are always thinking about the body, comparing themselves with others and with the perfect images presented by the media. Eventually, imagined imperfections like a tooth or a nose or a sprinkling of freckles become so exaggerated that they seem to fill the mirror. How could anyone find you attractive with teeth like that? Who would ever give you a job?

"Take your first step in the natural process of becoming your best," urges a Southern California medical center, "– successful, active, self-assured – *because life looks better when you do.*" The "first step" in this "natural process" turns out to be cosmetic surgery – and the advertisement is aimed at men, who now account for an eighth of all cosmetic surgery procedures and almost a third of all new facial cosmetic surgery.

As often, if this is a trend, California seems to be leading it. "I'm seeing a thousand percent more men now than I did ten years ago," says a plastic surgeon in Beverly Hills. His explanation is illuminating: "The general public began to ask, 'What can I spend money on that is nonspiritual that will give me that kind of satisfaction?'"

If the proportion of men turning to cosmetic surgery is increasing, perhaps women are becoming better educated on the issue. Women's magazines and other popular journals have been exposing the terrible dangers that often show up later – perhaps several years later – when these surgical procedures backfire, and an attempt to bolster security by manipulating physical appearance turns into an ugly nightmare.

When the human being is considered to be physical, every problem gets a physical interpretation and a physical "solution." This happens not only in medicine, but in much less appropriate places. I have been reading lately about sex "therapy," which is resorted to when problems in a relationship between man and woman are blamed on sex. Without hesitation I can say that sex is almost never the cause; sexual difficulties are the symptom. The problem is self-will – the overriding drive of "me, me, me" which cannot help manipulating, competing with, and offending others. Self-will invariably provokes resentment, and wherever there is resentment, reservation, or fear, a person's sexual responses are naturally affected adversely, for very good reason. Stirring up physical passions in the hope of changing such responses not only cannot solve the problem, it is likely to make it worse.

As long as one or both persons in a relationship is driven by self-will, no amount of physical counseling is going to solve their problems. On the other hand, if even one partner can begin to reduce his or her self-will, the other person cannot help responding. Tenderness comes, respect deepens, and sexual relations fall into harmonious place. It may take time, but this approach works where physical solutions often only add one problem to another. Otherwise, we are in the position of someone who takes to drinking to relieve stress. After a while, instead of one problem we have two: a stress problem and an alcohol problem.

Tragically, it is those who are most concerned with physical satisfactions and appearances who are most subject to what time does to both. During youth, when most people look their best, it may feel reassuring to gaze at yourself in the mirror and dwell on your appearance. But dwelling on one's appearance is a habit that bedevils even attractive teenagers, and there is very little to look forward to. After a certain middle point in life, the body *has* to show change. Wrinkles come, and then gray hairs; bags and crow's-feet fight for prominent positions beneath the eyes. Then the mirror is not a place for pleasure but for pain: nagging, insidious little questions that seem to say, "You ain't what you used to be." But by then the mirror habit has been formed. Unless you learn to get beneath the surface of consciousness and change your ways of thinking, the insecurity of the teenage years will stay to haunt you as you move into middle age.

And underneath all this, ever present but seldom expressed, is the biggest anxiety of all: the fear of physical deterioration, and of the last great change called death. "It's not so much that I'm afraid of being dead," friends with AIDS have told me. "It's *dying* that I'm afraid of – watching my body wither and waste away until I'm kept alive by machines and I'm not much more than a vegetable." I reassure them, "You can lift the burden of that fear completely through the practice of meditation, as you learn to identify less and less with the physical body and more and more with your real Self." Some of them have taken up the challenge, and nothing is more rewarding to me than to hear them say later with quiet assurance, "You were right. That fear is gone."

All in all, this idea "I am the body" is such a limited view of who we are! The body has to be imperfect; that is the nature of the physical world. Even the most beautiful body can only do so much and look so good. Sooner or later it is bound to age, develop wrinkles, grow ill, and eventually die. These things are certain. Yet we define who we are, what we can do, the relationships we have, even what we think and value and spend our lives on, in terms of this limited physical frame! We think we're going downhill when our body is past its prime, despite the evidence of countless men and women whose contribution to history was made in the second half of life. We think we are handicapped when our body is handicapped, although one look at Stephen Hawking, the brilliant physicist who can scarcely move or speak in his wheelchair because of neural deterioration, should convince anyone that the human being is much, much more than the physical body. And – which is really much the same thing – we think we are handicapped by adverse conditions outside us, though most great accomplishments in life can only have been made by overcoming obstacles. Even Gross's greatest physical achievements are essentially due to Subtle: the triumph of inner strength over the apparent limitations of the laws of physics. Gross may get the Olympic gold, but Subtle deserves the glory.

Hypersensitivity

As the insecurity of body-identification grows, we become increasingly sensitive to external appearances. Everything has to be the way we like it. As we go on splitting hairs about what we like and dislike, the range of what we can tolerate grows more and more constricted. Finally nothing is satisfactory; everything is somehow wrong. When you go out for ice cream, none of the hundred and thirty-seven flavors is quite right. Nobody makes proper shoes any more, the weather is always too hot or too cold, your friends consistently let you down. Things are always too short, too long, too wet, too dry, too bright, too salty, too dull, too scratchy. It is a familiar state to many people today.

Most of us are subject to this in some degree. For some, a vague insecurity is the usual state. Others just have their little ways in which things have to be right.

I had a friend in India who used to take me for breakfast to a rather exclusive British establishment which had its own particular way of setting a table. Unfortunately, my friend had a different way, and since he couldn't abide the thought of things being done wrong by people who ought to know better, as soon as we sat down he would systematically rearrange everything – cutlery, glasses, napkins, chairs, even the salt and pepper shakers – while the waiters stood at a respectful distance exchanging meaningful looks. Once, to help him, I suggested that he try to sit through one whole breakfast without changing anything. His face put on a tortured expression. "I *can't,*" he said. "You might as well ask me to go out without my socks."

This is not a harmless mental state; it can have undesirable effects. I remember an event from the early days of our meditation center, when we had just rented a small church in Berkeley for my weekly talks. The church was on Parker Street just off Telegraph Avenue, where the action was in the mid-sixties; so we drew a good crowd. After a few weeks, to enable more people to see better, we moved the chairs to run the length of the room rather than the width. That evening an earnest young man showed up who had been telling me that meditation was what he had been looking for all his life. He took one look inside, saw the chairs running the long way instead of the short, and ran out shaking his head and muttering, "Crazy. Crazy! *Crazy!*" His mind was so upset that it would not allow him even to sit down and listen. I couldn't help feeling sorry for him, because life holds us hostage when we are hypersensitive to physical appearances in a world of constant change.

Perhaps more than any other single emotional factor, it is this exaggerated sensitivity to the physical level of life that prompts us to overreact to our surroundings in ways that bring on emotional and physical distress: anger, resentment, competitiveness, anxiety, greed, jealousy, depression, loneliness, fear. All these mental states impose stress on the mind and body. And in addition to stress, negative mental states like these seem to be associated with illness in other ways as well – affecting, for example, how well the immune system functions.

The reason for this connection is simple, though perhaps difficult to grasp. The more we think of ourselves as physical, the more we take things physically, passing to the body our emotional states and personal interpretations of life around us. Body-identification is the emotional bridge by which agitation in the mind is transferred to disturbances in the body.

So-called psychosomatic disorders are only part of this. The person who identifies with the body sees *everything* physically. Inner needs get a physical interpretation, so that an emotional emptiness, for example, becomes a drive to eat or smoke or experience some sensation. And external events and other people are seen as personal challenges or even threats.

This is much, much more common than we realize. Everyone knows, for example, that "Sticks and stones can break my bones but

names can never hurt me"; but when someone starts making oppro-
brious remarks about us, our hormones start pumping adrenaline as
if we were cave men with an angry tiger in our path. Why? There is
no physical threat, but we take it physically – unless we are one of
those rare individuals who are secure enough to shrug off words for
what they are. Left to his own, Gross Body would not even notice
being called names. It is Subtle that takes it personally and makes
Gross respond – unless, of course, we do not identify ourselves
with our physical frame.

There are interesting parallels here with some kinds of allergy,
which is a physical hypersensitivity – an acute overreaction of the
immune system to a particular physical irritant. The irritant varies
from person to person, and so does the area of hypersensitivity.
Some people are allergic to penicillin, and their skin breaks out in a
rash. Others show no reaction to penicillin; their Waterloo is pollen,
which causes violent irritation in the nose. And in a few, the reaction is not confined to the irritated area but explodes all over the
body, so that from a relatively minor event, such as a bee sting, the
whole organism goes into sometimes fatal shock.

Many immunologists – probably most – will argue that the
body's response to an allergen is entirely physical and chemical in
nature. For unknown reasons, the immune system attacks a harmless substance that should pass unnoticed. However, emotional
stimuli too can trigger an allergic response, suggesting that the hypersensitivity can involve not just Gross but Subtle as well.

It is interesting to observe that the very substances which produce the symptoms of allergy, such as histamine and bradykinin,
are also released in an attack of anger. This may be more than coincidence. The person who gets angry easily – or, for that matter,
annoyed, frustrated, jealous, or upset – *is* hypersensitive. Something perceived as provocative produces not only an emotional
response in the mind but physiological reactions in the body. In the
case of allergy, too, the *perception* of an irritant can trigger an attack, even if the irritant itself is absent. And if the mind has linked

the allergic reaction with a particular emotional response, the emotional stimulus alone can provoke an attack. In children with bronchial asthma, for example, relief often comes when an emotionally involved parent is temporarily removed from the scene.

I read, too, about a man allergic to zucchini who went to a friend's for dinner and enjoyed the meal thoroughly. Then his hostess, who knew about his problem with this innocuous squash, asked if he had had any difficulty with the food.

"Oh, no," he replied. "It was delicious. Why?"

"Because," she said, "I put zucchini in the casserole. I just wanted to see if you could tell."

The man broke into a violent rash. But the real surprise was yet to come: she had not really put zucchini in at all.

In one famous case of hay fever, a doctor provoked a violent attack by merely showing his patient a rose. Then he showed her that the flower was not real, but simply a well-made imitation. With no possibility of pollen, it was evident that it was the mind that had triggered the alarm. That insight must have been enough to break the conditioning, because on her next visit she brought in a real rose, buried her nose in it, and breathed in deeply several times to show her doctor she was cured.

No one understands why the body's defenses, ordinarily so efficient, suddenly become obsessed by imaginary threats. But we do know now, thanks to researchers like Robert Ader and Candace Pert, that there is constant communication between the immune system and the brain, and that the immune system can be conditioned by how the brain interprets an experience. We know how Gothic heroines can fall prey to delusions; here it is as if the ethereal Mrs. Subtle, walking too much on the moors in her private world, suddenly focuses paranoid fears on some harmless specks. "Gross," she warns, "beware of pollens! They're all around us, seeking to do us harm."

"Come on," says Gross, who is biochemically oriented. "Who's afraid of a little pollen?"

But Subtle knows who is in command. "Gross," she warns, "you'd just better do as I say." She has linked something harmless with the need for self-defense, and when she perceives a threat, Gross attacks.

I want to make it clear that I am not at all suggesting that allergy is simply "in one's head." The physical problem is not imagined but very real. What is intriguing about allergy in a discussion of mind and body is the instances in which the two appear to have become linked through a process of conditioning, so that the body's response can be triggered by the way the mind "sees."

Some years ago I read about a woman who had become so fearful of someone breaking into her house at night that she got a gun to keep under her pillow. Every evening she lay down to sleep half expecting someone to break in. Naturally, when she awoke one night to a noise at her bedroom window and saw a shadowy figure outside, she pulled out the weapon and fired. She swore later that she *did* see a person there, but the real offender was only a lilac branch in the wind.

I suspect that there is an analogous situation whenever the mind is involved in a pathologic process. Gross may fire the shot, but the person with the itchy trigger finger is his hypersensitive companion. What Subtle sees is what Gross responds to — even if what she sees is not really there.

Mind and Illness

In effect, this moves the center of influence in our lives to events *outside* us. Interpreting life as physical, we give so much importance to external circumstances that we finally lose all touch with an inner self. Everything that we think matters lies in the world outside us, and the desperate cry of our inner needs — to love, to give, to belong — goes unheard.

This is really just the insecurity of body-identification again, and people try to deal with it in very different ways. An aggressive person, for example, may try to compensate by seeking to dominate the world outside him, manipulating events and people to gain control over a sphere of security where he will not feel threatened. Many people we do not think of as insecure fit this category, including individuals with the "Type A" personality pattern that cardiologist Meyer Friedman and others have shown to be highly prone to heart attack.

The clinical characteristics of Type A suggest a personality that is obsessively concerned with the physical level of life. "Type A behavior," Dr. Friedman explains, "is above all a continuous struggle . . . to accomplish or achieve more and more things . . . in less and less time, frequently in the face of opposition – real or imagined – from other persons." Type A's are driven by an aggressive need to compete and to dominate, and they measure their success and status in physical tokens which they are constantly comparing with others': not only their golf score and how much money they make, but how many stamps they have in their collection, how many facts they know, how much work they can do in a day or an hour, how many things they can do at once – almost anything, in fact, that can be counted.

For this reason, the Type A person characteristically shows a particular kind of time-driven behavior. Dr. Friedman calls the pattern "hurry sickness": the compulsive need to fit more and more activities into less and less time, often for no reason except to *do* more. This reaches such ridiculous extremes as conducting business while driving in rush-hour traffic, or reading several magazines while eating lunch and maintaining a telephone conversation at the same time.

All these traits Dr. Friedman traces to a root insecurity for which the Type A personality tries to compensate by dominating the world outside him. Such a person, Dr. Friedman and his colleagues observe, has very little awareness of an inner self, and even less sensitivity to the needs of those around him.

As Type A behavior becomes extreme, it is characteristic that little, external things assume monstrous proportions. Losing a golf game, paying too much for a cup of coffee, or having to wait while the person ahead of you at the cash register fumbles in his pocket for change – all these, for the Type A, are highly provocative events. Anger is the typical outcome, and nothing is too trifling to provoke it. (Dr. Friedman describes two Type A men having a livid argument over the proper way to install a roll of toilet paper.) For such a person, everything is a personal challenge throughout the day. The result is perhaps the most highly disease-prone characteristic of the Type A personality: what Dr. Friedman calls a "free-floating hostility" that is ready to erupt in violent words or even actions over virtually anything at all.

"What's frightening," Dr. Friedman observed recently, "is how much the environment is nourishing Type A behavior now." This is a very important observation. I see Type A behavior everywhere I go, and not only among business people but among students and teachers and mothers; and it is much, much more common today, much more acceptable and even encouraged, than it was when Drs. Friedman and Rosenman introduced the concept in 1973. This is a frightening development not merely because of the implications for heart attack; it is ominous for the whole society. I have seen one motorist in San Francisco get out of his car and attack another for honking at him when the traffic light turned green, and it is not uncommon to read in the papers that someone has been shot or forced into an accident on the highway because someone did not like the way he or she was driving. So-called meaningless violence is frequent in our cities; and even in our schools, a child may be shot because of the kind of shoes she wears or the color of his jacket.

After many years of research, Dr. Friedman believes that he can trace a plausible connection between the Type A mental state and the physiology of heart disease – that is, actual links in a causal chain between mind and body. And the initial link, the provoking cause, is the way the Type A person views himself in the world around him.

Since the Type A person perceives his daily environment as a physical challenge – a challenge he must overcome to survive – his body is kept flooded by hormones like norepinephrine and ACTH that rouse it for a physical struggle. (High blood levels of

ACTH, Dr. Friedman comments, are characteristic not only of Type A's but of Columbia River salmon during their long upstream battle to spawn, after which they die in a state of cardiovascular exhaustion.) One of the purposes of these "struggle hormones" is to divert blood to organs like the heart and lungs. This is ordinarily an emergency measure. But when the body is kept chronically aroused for aggressive action, other organ systems are deprived of normal blood flow. In time, the liver loses the ability to remove fats from the blood, and cholesterol and triglycerides build up rapidly in the blood vessels. Arteriosclerosis and heart disease follow.

There are interesting similarities here with more general ways in which the body responds to psychological stress. When the brain decides that the organism is being challenged, it initiates a large number of biochemical signals to rouse the body, one of which releases ACTH into the blood stream to stimulate the production of the "struggle hormones" epinephrine and norepinephrine. Dr. Friedman is careful to distinguish his conjectured Type A response from the general biochemistry of stress, but there are common elements: a physiological arousal that puts great strain on the body if maintained, triggered by the mind's perception of a threat in the world outside.

Whatever the biochemistry, Type A behavior is statistically linked very strongly with heart disease – more strongly, in fact, than cholesterol and dietary fat. Clearly, however much a high-fat diet increases the risk of heart disease, Gross fat is evidently only part of the problem. Subtle has a kind of fat problem too, and it leaves Gross open not only to heart disease but to other breakdowns in health as well. For there is more and more evidence that not only the Type A personality but negative mental states in general have a destructive effect on physical well-being.

If Gross is what he eats, Subtle is what she thinks. And just as there are "junk foods" and nutritious foods, there are junk-food and healthful states of mind. My friend Laurel is always singing the praises of homemade, whole-grain bread. Patience is like a slice of Laurel's bread; it nourishes the mind in at least a dozen ways.

Impatience, anger, hostility, and resentment, on the other hand, are like those roasted nuts you sometimes find in a department store: salty, stale, and predisposing to high blood pressure if indulged in excessively. And a sweet, gooey piece of self-will – doing something you want just because you want to, the way you want to, when you want to, although it benefits nobody including yourself – is like a big slice of cheesecake. There is nothing like cheesecake for putting on pounds, and nothing like indulging self-will for making the ego obese.

Extra pounds are not put on the body with two or three huge meals. We grow fat through nibbling: a little of this, a little of that, twenty-five times a day. Subtle snacks too: a bit of resentment after breakfast, some hostility for high tea, a handful of anxious attitudes before bed. She even indulges in midnight snacks, as most of us can attest when we recall our dreams. Thoughts may not supply calories, but when we go on thinking about ourselves like this day and night – "I want this; I don't like that; that's not fair; life's not being nice to me" – by the end of a year the ego will have put on enough pounds to warrant a place in *Ripley's Believe It or Not*.

An overweight ego is touchy, acutely sensitive to little things. It becomes rigid, takes everything personally, and is offended as easily as it gets inflated – all of which make it extremely vulnerable to what life hands out, and prone to anger when it feels its demands are not met. When Gross is overweight, he finds it stressful even to climb a flight of stairs. Subtle, too, when she gets bloated by negative states of mind, makes stress of even little things, simply because she views them as big and takes them personally.

Most people find change stressful, so I do not find it surprising that researchers have discovered a statistical relation between falling ill and the experience of major "life events" such as the death of a spouse, getting married or divorced, and losing a job. When the psychiatrists Richard Rahe and Thomas Holmes ranked some of these events on a scale from major to relatively minor, they found that those who have experienced a higher index of such changes generally report a greater incidence of ill health.

Yet most of us find that this doesn't quite tally with experience. Are we supposed to avoid change if we want good health? Few of us would find that appealing, and it doesn't seem to make sense. All around us we see people who seem to thrive on change, while others living tedious, humdrum lives seem almost likely to fall ill.

Reasoning similarly, Richard Lazarus of the University of California at Berkeley pursued a different line of research, and found a strong statistical correlation between breakdowns in health and the cumulative effect of what he calls "hassles" – the thousand little daily irritations, insignificant in themselves, that sometimes seem to build up until the thousand-and-first makes mind and body scream, "I can't take any more!"

But again, this is a statistical conclusion – a generalization. Some individuals feel hassled by everything, while others seem able to cope with whatever life brings them. The difference must lie somehow in how change is perceived; and I suspect that what makes the difference is not so much whether change is interpreted as stressful, but whether it is viewed as a personal threat. It is natural to feel challenged by change, but it is certainly not necessary for the body to meet every change with a hormonal response of "fight or flight." The insecure mind greets change with an unconscious question: "Is this something I can cope with?" If the answer is no, whether rightly or wrongly, that event is seen as overwhelming, "one more thing I can't handle."

Dr. Arthur Schmale of the University of Rochester speaks of two mental states that seem fruitful ground for illness. Where an aggressive personality like Type A meets the events of daily life in a constant struggle for control, a different personality – perhaps even the same person at a later stage in life – responds by giving up. For both, I would say, it is outside events that are calling the tune. But in the second person there is no longer any attempt to dance. What happens to that person is felt to be beyond control, and no sense of inner resources remains for meeting the challenge. Such a person may feel an empty shell, with nothing inside at all.

This response to life is perhaps the most tragic consequence of body-identification, and the two states of mind that characterize it are helplessness and hopelessness. When these states of mind are chronic, the body's capacity to resist illness and to mobilize recovery often seems impaired, perhaps because the immune system itself is weakened. Where an aggressive mind rouses the body's defenses over everything, the mind that feels helpless and hopeless scarcely bothers to mobilize at all for a struggle it feels bound to lose.

By contrast, the psychologist Suzanne Kobasa has identified three traits of what she calls a "hardy personality" – one with the capacity to "buffer the negative effects of stress." These traits are her "three C's": challenge, commitment, and control. A hardy person feels commitment to something that he or she values deeply, views change as a challenge rather than a threat, and feels "a sense of personal control over one's life" – all, I would say, qualities that can only be sustained when a person has a sense of being more than just a physical creature.

The most stressful of the "life events" on the Holmes-Rahe scale is the death of a spouse, and researchers have found that bereavement takes a severe toll on health – so severe, in fact, that the surviving partner often dies within a year or two of the loss, as if weakened by the stress of the event. But although everyone finds bereavement stressful, we expect a "hardy personality" to rebound after a period of grief when she has something to live for. Such a person survives bereavement and every other blow life deals her because she has a reason to live. Again, this is the mind's contribution, not the body's. The human being needs meaning in order to live, and meaning cannot come from events outside us. It can only come from within: from the way we see the world, informed by wisdom, compassion, understanding, love, and trust.

This deep-seated human need for meaning and purpose may go unnoticed in our earlier years, when the body is young and life's physical challenges and rewards engage our zest for living. But the need becomes acute when the physical level begins to fail us. This occurs when we lose someone we love or depend on, or when we feel deprived of any crutch we have been leaning on in the world outside us. But it also occurs, inevitably, when the body ages, as we lose our physical attractiveness and our capacity for physical prowess and enjoyment. If we do not have something to live for then, frustration with life can only mount, and helplessness and hopelessness, the last and most destructive of life's stresses, are bound to follow.

Changing the Mind

Fortunately, all of these mental states can be changed. In their Recurrent Coronary Prevention program, Meyer Friedman and Diane Ulmer have demonstrated that even a severely Type A person can draw on the very drives that threaten his life to remake himself into a "Type B," calm, compassionate, and vital with the joy of living. If behavioral training can do so much, I believe there is much more that can be accomplished when one learns to make changes from within the mind. Even a person severely afflicted with helplessness and hopelessness can be transformed, as I have experienced personally with persons suffering from HIV disease and cancer. Fortunately, even a little of an inner discipline like meditation acts swiftly to restore one's sense of self and self-control. Once that comes, hope follows, and the capacity to deal with one's illness often improves dramatically.

When people hear about the role of the mind in illness, one of the unfortunate misunderstandings is to think, "So I'm to blame for getting sick?" I never want to give that impression. It is absurd and debilitating to raise the question of blame. For me the important message is completely positive: Whatever your physical situation, your mind can help you to deal with it if you train your mind to be forgiving, compassionate, calm, and kind. "You can have no better friend," the Buddha says, "than a well-trained mind – and no worse enemy than an untrained mind."

Physical problems like illness are often like the red warning light on the dashboard of a car. When your car is low on oil, a little red light goes on; when your mind is low on security, you may develop peptic ulcer. Every stab of pain is a red warning, an appeal from the body that something is wrong.

Imagine Mr. and Mrs. Body having trouble with their car. "Gross, dear," Subtle says, "that little red light on the dash is on again."

"What little red light?" says Gross absent-mindedly. He is busy watching television, and there is only seven minutes left of play. "Did you remember to take out the key?"

After the game is over, with a lot of prodding, Gross gets up and takes his tools out to the car. When he finally comes back, his hands are grimy but his face is shining. "Honey," he announces proudly, "that little light'll never bother you again!"

"Oh, Gross! What did you do?"

"Just took it out. Here, you can keep it if you like. Of course, you'd better be careful about checking the oil every time you go out. No telling now when it might be low."

Whenever we treat the symptoms of an illness, we may be removing the red light. Of course, treating symptoms is vitally important. But it is good to remember that the purpose of the light is communication. In this sense, we may look on many physical ailments as urgent messages from Subtle: "I'm constantly in stress; I keep putting myself under pressure. If you don't help me soon, it's going to damage Gross's heart."

I once saw a detective movie dedicated to "all those who got away with it." The one who always gets away with it is the mind. The body is almost never the real cause of physical problems. As Dr. Friedman says of heart disease, "Diet and cigarettes may be the bullets, but behavior is the gun" – and the mind, I would add, is the one that pulls the trigger. When we identify with the body, Subtle acts out her problems and Gross pays the penalties. There is a saying in my mother tongue: "The drum gets the beating and the drummer gets the cash."

Once you see this, you develop a very understanding attitude toward the body. It is not its fault if our mental states are negative, and there is no point in punishing ourselves for it either. For this reason I am on very friendly terms with my body, which I call my buddy. I never inflict any kind of harsh training on it in the name of self-discipline. All my effort has gone into training the mind, which is the very opposite of asceticism. When the mind is well trained, to paraphrase Suzanne Kobasa, it feels committed, confident, and in control. It scarcely interferes with the body at all, leaving the body free to protect and heal itself – a job at which Gross excels, as any doctor will tell you.

But this state cannot be attained by any amount of external manipulation. To make such changes, we need to go deep into the field of forces that is the mind.

Chapter Five

A Field of Forces

B IOLOGISTS TELL US that the body is composed of thousands of chemical compounds, many of them quite complex. Yama would have a more concise but equally practical answer: Gross Body, he would say, is made out of food. From the same perspective, Subtle is a highly complex field of forces, all made out of prana.

These forces, of course, are not perceptible, any more than gravitation is. But just as we infer the properties of physical forces from effects we can observe, the effects of subtle forces on our lives make it possible to describe their workings in a scientific manner.

Once our village high school teacher explained the field of forces around a magnet: something we could not see, but which was as real as the magnet itself. "Would you like to see the invisible?" he asked dramatically. With the flair of a magician, he dusted a light layer of iron filings onto a sheet of paper and brought the magnet up underneath. Before our eyes, the filings shifted to make two big oval swirls. "Imagine that all around the magnet," he said triumphantly. *"That* is what magnetism looks like."

By the same criteria, we can "see" the forces that make up Subtle too. Desires, compulsions, rigid likes and dislikes, are all powerful forces; with a little detachment, we can actually feel them push us into directions where we do not want to go, very much like a bully pushing a smaller child off the road.

Or look at hostility. Just like magnetism, it has specific, predictable effects. The next time you find yourself going around with a chip on your shoulder, sit down with a group of friends. Don't join in; just sit there, as if to say, "Impress me." Whatever they say, do not laugh. If you have to speak, be sarcastic. Just as a magnet polarizes filings, your mood will set in motion a wave of irritation that rearranges people's feelings as it spreads. One of your friends may go home and curse the cat; another will quarrel with her partner, a third will set his bartender's teeth on edge. The field *is* there; if we know what to look for, we can almost see its shape in people's lives.

Similarly, these forces shape our own lives, even at the physical level; for the balance of forces in the mind has an intimate relationship with health. In the long run, I suspect, an unstable mind is very likely to bring on physical problems – just as a stable mind, a tranquil mind, generally preserves health and enhances recovery.

Prana and Health

On the most general level, the key to this is prana. Prana is undifferentiated energy. Just as the subtle body underlies the physical, prana underlies all the expressions of physical energy with which we are familiar: electromagnetic energy, gravitation, and the forces within the nucleus of the atom. The body hums with prana, for this is the power that sustains the millions of events which enable us to stretch out our hands or open our eyes. Furthermore, when we open our eyes, it is prana that enables us to see. Just as an electric bulb will light up only when electricity passes through it, the senses perceive only when prana is present.

But prana is not physical; it is also the energy of the mind. We know what force desire has; a powerful desire can lead us into a bakery against our will, make a man walk a mile for a particular kind of carcinogen. The force behind desire is prana. When we love, reason, worry, resolve conflicts, choose, show patience, or exercise the will, we draw on prana. The implication is highly practical: body and mind draw on the very same power. When all the forces of the mind are in harmonious balance, we function at optimum health. But when this balance is thrown off – say, in habitually trying to satisfy a particular kind of conditioned desire – the balance of prana is thrown off in the body too. If this imbalance is prolonged, part of the body begins to suffer.

In this connection, it is interesting to see the role prana plays in physical health during the stages of sleep. While we are awake, prana circulates throughout the body and senses. But in dreaming, it is withdrawn from the body and senses into the mind. We do not hear, see, smell, taste, or feel; though there is still prana in the circuitry, the senses have all been unplugged. Gross Body is dead to the world, but ethereal Subtle is sitting up by lantern light going over all her old impressions, arranging and rearranging them to suit her hopes, desires, and fears. If you get up after eight hours' sleep and feel you have been working all night, you probably have. Subtle has been up and busy, burning the midnight prana.

In dreamless sleep, however, even the mind is still. Prana is withdrawn from the subtle body too, into the very core of personality. In physiological terms, this is when the nervous system rests, when the body repairs itself and the mind is refreshed. In profound meditation we enter this state wakefully, and this process of healing and rejuvenation goes on at a very deep level in both body and mind.

At the moment of conception, each of us comes into life with a particular packet of prana to last us until death. In a sense, a prana checking account is opened in our name as our legacy in this life. We can draw on this account as we choose; but when it is gone, the vitality in this body comes to an end, as surely as a light goes out when the power is switched off.

To live *is* to spend prana; there we have no choice. But we do have a choice in what to spend our prana on. By some strange law of subtle physics, it is not the body that consumes prana most; it is the mind. The physical act of seeing, for example, uses very little prana. But look at a gambler watching a roulette wheel; you can almost see prana pouring from the eyes. Selfish desire throws open our senses, and prana gushes out.

Abundant prana means greater resilience, greater reserves of energy for weathering the storms and stress of life. To this extent there may be some connection with what Dr. Hans Selye, a brilliant pioneer in stress research, called "adaptation energy." Every organism, Selye observed, has a particular capacity for adapting to stress in its environment. If a laboratory rat is left in extreme cold, for example, its body soon learns to adjust to its new conditions by burning food more efficiently and losing less heat through the skin. Once these mechanisms have been acquired, it is able to adapt to still colder conditions where a normal rat would perish. If it gets enough food, Selye asked, should it not be able to go on resisting low temperatures indefinitely? Yet strangely enough, after a few months, resistance fails; after that it cannot withstand even a small drop in temperature from the normal. Physical energy, calories, is still adequate, but something else – "adaptation energy" – has run out. Selye does not try to explain this; he simply observes. But much the same is true for prana too.

Of course, if you live in a smog-polluted world, you can have a lot of prana and still succumb to lung disease. If you play football in your eighties, you can still break a leg. In such cases all prana can do is give you more resistance, keep your bones more pliable – and, when prana is abundant, mobilize the body's capacity for healing itself.

"The length of the human life span," Dr. Selye commented, "appears to be primarily determined by the amount of available adaptation energy." Again, substitute "prana" and I think this is quite correct – except that it is not only the amount, but also how rapidly that amount is consumed. When we have some control over the forces of the mind, prana is conserved and vitality greatly extended.

One implication of this is quite important: there is no necessary connection between vitality and age. Many people today, including physicians, believe that senility is unavoidable, since the physiological effects of aging and decay affect the brain. It is worth repeating that this assumption is not quite correct. You may not be able to climb Mount Everest or swim seventy Olympic laps when you are eighty-one; this I concede. The body is physical, and any vehicle begins to wear with age. But I am talking about the driver. Even in your eighties you can have a clear mind, sound judgment, and a powerful will – if you have prana.

Conversely, senility is not confined to old age. To be a fogey you do not have to be old; you simply have to have a rigid mind. With the kind of life many people lead today, they may not have to wait until retirement; senility can begin in the thirties and forties. Where prana is present, body and mind are active and resilient; otherwise, rigor mortis sets in in both.

If you have a million dollars in the bank, it does not bother you to lose a dollar or two. It is the same when you have immense reserves of prana. At the time of his death, it is said, Mahatma Gandhi was worth only two dollars in material possessions, but he was a prana billionaire. He spent his life like a billionaire too, gave his vitality freely to all. Since the age of twenty-four, when he went to South Africa as a highly unpromising lawyer, Gandhi spent prana right and left to ease people's burdens and help resolve their conflicts.

Don't financiers say that to make money, you have to spend it? Gandhi spent prana to generate it in others, and he generated so much that for the first time in history, a nation that had been exploited for three hundred years was able, without violence, to shake off the domination of the greatest empire the world had seen – and not in enmity, but in friendship.

People whose bank account is in two figures, on the other hand, worry all the way through the supermarket. They count everything, keep a running total, weigh each little item against the others. Similarly, when prana is dwindling, you become insecure, vacillating, defensive, wide open to the stress of life.

Nothing is more tragic than to be down-and-out in prana. Prana brings fire to a person, brightness, brilliance, vigor, health, sensitivity. When prana is overdrawn, usually through indulging self-centered desires, the latter part of life becomes sorrowful indeed. The desires are still there, but the capacity to satisfy them is gone. In those who have played with their senses too much, especially with sex, you can almost see the eyes lose their brightness, the skin its glow, the voice its timbre; the whole personality seems to be covered with a pall.

Without any moral judgment, I cannot pass through the streets of the Tenderloin district in San Francisco without a stab of pity for those I see – men and women whose prana has been consumed, yet whose desires and addictions remain. The signs and advertisements there have a different message for me. "Put down your vitality, your creativity, your resistance to disease, and we'll give you a few minutes of excitement. If it doesn't satisfy you, come on back – but don't be surprised if the price is higher."

Body and Mind

When we talk about emotional states and physical health, we usually say that the mind "does something" to the body. Anger causes the heart to race, fear releases adrenalin, intense dislike may cause the skin to break out in hives. But in fact, the distinction between body and mind is not much more than a matter of linguistic convenience. These are not really two; they are one.

There is an analogy with the way physicists speak about matter and energy. If our eyes could see on a much finer scale, this book which seems so solid might look like a dazzling matrix of activity on the threshold between matter and energy. On this level there would be no place where book clearly left off and air began; book and air would be regions on a continuum, with an indistinct but definitely shared area in common. Similarly, there is no sharp division between body and mind. Gross and Subtle lie on a continuum of prana. If we see only the gross part of what we are, that is because of the limitations of our senses.

Anger, for example, is not simply a mental event. It is a whole constellation of events from emotional to physiological. Anger does not "cause" the mind to race, the nostrils to flare, and breathing to become disordered. It *is* flared nostrils, disordered breathing, excessive adrenalin, a racing mind, clouded judgment, and probably a thousand and one other factors, mental and physical, all at once.

With one tug, this perspective pulls the carpet out from under the mind-body problem. When we look at a person through physical glasses, we see Gross. If we could put on prana glasses – as in a sense we do, after years of meditation – we would see the same person as Subtle, a highly complex field of forces. The person is the same; we are distinguishing between two views.

In certain circles you will hear it said that we are punished for getting angry. The Buddha would use different language: we are punished *by* getting angry. Anger is its own punishment. When we fly into a rage, no celestial Lawgiver has to strike us down; we are cursing ourselves: "May I get an ulcer! May my blood pressure soar! May my heart be afflicted with ectopic beats!" It is a curse that never fails, because the emotion and its consequences are one.

I would go so far as to say that every movement in the mind has a physiological component. Every emotion is an event, or cluster of events, which takes place in mind and body together. It follows that every chronic or habitual mental state includes effects on health. Often these effects include the stress response, which Hans Selye defined as a general physiological arousal that activates defense mechanisms all over the body.

Blood pressure is one of these defense mechanisms, and it is controlled by several factors sensitive to emotional states. The autonomic nervous system, for example, increases or decreases blood pressure in response to emotional as well as physical demands. Similarly, blood pressure is increased when the blood vessels are constricted by hormones like epinephrine and norepinephrine, both of which are released during physical effort and psychological stress. A person who feels constantly under emotional stress might

84

well show high blood pressure, which then aggravates other physical problems.

Ordinarily we think of stress as caused by something outside us. But as we have seen, although Gross Body does the responding, it is Subtle, the mind, who interprets our environment and decides when our equilibrium is threatened. Stress is not caused so much by difficult conditions as by what we think of such conditions. Physical pain, of course, is stressful, but so is anything we *consider* painful or distressing. If it is stressful to receive a cut on the skin, it can be equally stressful to receive a cut in pay, or to be raked over the coals by our boss, or in fact to be put through anything we thoroughly, intensely dislike. In most cases, the world does not impose stress on us; we impose stress on ourselves.

Stress

In this sense, much of the relationship between mental states and physical health can be related directly to stress. By Dr. Selye's definition, stress is the body's response to any demanding change in environment – a precise syndrome of defense mechanisms by which the body tries to adapt to its new conditions. If these conditions are unrelieved, however, this response may become habitual. Over a period of time, one of the bodily systems may break down at its weakest point, precipitating what Dr. Selye calls a "disease of adaptation."

If I may paraphrase the Buddha, "Not to have what we want is stressful; to have what we do not want is stressful." In daily living, what brings on stress is often no more or less than our strong, self-centered desires and self-will – the fierce need to have what we want when we want it, and in the way we want it too. If you look at anyone who seems chronically under stress, you will often find that person subject to rigid likes and dislikes which he or she cannot stand to have thwarted.

Dr. John Hunter, an English surgeon with a reputation for having tightly-held opinions, used to complain, "My life is at the mercy of any rascal who chooses to annoy me." It was no exaggeration.

When a colleague contradicted him during a medical board meeting, Hunter stopped speaking, left the room, and fell dead from a heart attack into the arms of a fellow physician.

In a much smaller way, this applies to all of us. Imagine, even our blood pressure can be regulated by others! They say something irritating, but it is our arteries that respond.

At the Menninger Clinic in Kansas, a yogi from India has repeatedly demonstrated under laboratory conditions that he has the capacity to perform all kinds of tricks with his nervous system: slow and speed up his heart at will, push his blood pressure up to two hundred fifty in a couple of minutes, and many others. I do not believe he is trying to show off; he is simply demonstrating to the scientific community, in a way they can appreciate, that there is much more to the relationship between body and mind than meets the eye.

You do not have to be a yogi to produce such effects. The next time you find yourself getting angry – or, for that matter, watching some passionate scene in the movies – keep one finger on your pulse. Right there in the Plaza Theater, in just two minutes, your heart will begin to race. The question is not whether the mind can regulate physiology, but whether we can regulate the mind.

Many people who have followed spiritual disciplines – particularly in India, where this has long been systematized as a science – will testify that to some extent, the autonomic nervous system itself can be brought under conscious control. Biofeedback experiments support the same conclusion. My own approach, however, is rather different. Instead of trying to control the physiology of specific organs, I prefer learning to control the mind. Just as Dr. Hunter's mind was conditioned to become angry at the slightest provocation, so any mind can be taught to become patient. When your mind is calm, patient, and compassionate, you do not respond to life with anger. Your blood pressure is not affected by an insult; your heart does not race when you are contradicted; all the vital functions of the body keep their appropriate pace. This is the kind of control I am interested in, for it has a direct bearing on living in full health, free from rigidity and destructive ways of thinking.

A Field of Forces

To understand how this can be accomplished, we need to look more closely at the field of forces that is the mind. Taken individually, these forces are called *samskaras*. What we think of as personality is a dynamic interplay of samskaras, differing from person to person but essentially alike in how they work. I know of no concept more powerful or more practical, for samskaras are the key to how problems in personality can be solved.

Put simply, a samskara is a conditioned, automatic way of thinking and responding to the events of life around us. When a samskara is strong, we think of it as a fixed part of a person's personality. Othello is jealous, Hamlet indecisive, Macbeth ambitious; that, we say, is their nature. To many biologists, this is something that is built into our very genes. But the samskaras themselves – jealousy, vacillation, competition – are not permanent mental furniture; they are a process. A samskara is a thought repeated over and over a thousand times, leading to words repeated a thousand times, resulting in action repeated a thousand times. At the beginning it is only a burgeoning habit of thought; you do not necessarily act on it. But once it becomes rigid, a samskara dictates behavior. It begins as a conditioned habit in the mind and grows into conditioned behavior.

Resentment, for example, is a powerful samskara. It does not burst full-blown into the mind; it grows. At first you simply expect people to behave towards you in a particular way. If they behave in their own way instead, you get surprised, then irritated. The samskara is digging its little channel in consciousness. In the early stages, this channel may be only an inch or so deep. Thought may flow down it, but it may also flow somewhere else. Also, the walls are still soft and crumbly; they may cave in and fill the channel a little – for example, when someone you dislike says something kind. There is an element of choice. But every time we respond to a situation with resentment, the channel gets a little deeper. It is almost neurological; we are conditioning the patterns of thinking within the brain. And finally there is a huge Grand Canal in the mind. Then anything at all is enough to provoke a conditioned re-sentful response. Consciousness pours down the sluice of least re-sistance, and resentment simply seethes.

When a samskara is dug down to bedrock, the construction crew begins to make it a monument for posterity. This is dwelling on the samskara – going over your files of resentment, reviewing your fantasies, replaying old records of bygone times. Every time you do this, you cement another tile or two in the samskara-channel walls to make sure they will never crumble. Once the job is completed, that trait of personality has become rigid. Afterwards everyone in the world can be kind to you and you will still be hostile, resentful, or suspicious. You will not even recognize kindness for what it is; you will think people are making fun of you or trying to cheat you out of your money. And even when there is no provocation, at least a trickle of consciousness will be running down the sluiceway twenty-four hours a day.

Here etymology is revealing: *sam* means "intensely"; *kara* comes from the root meaning "to do." A samskara is always up and doing, continuously working away. Once it is established in the mind you do not have to think it; the samskara thinks itself. You dwell on it, brood on it constantly; you can think of nothing else. I have known people for whom sex was like this. Brooding on sexual enjoyment is one of the most powerful and most common of samskaras. If it becomes automatic, even when you are doing something else the thought of sex will be running along in con-sciousness beneath the surface level.

One fascinating part of this analysis is that the outside stimulus makes very little difference. A person with an anger samskara will get angry over anything; that is how his mind has been conditioned. In this sense, most of us have the freedom of a juke box. If I push a particular set of buttons at the juke box in Beasley's Restaurant I get a particular song, probably sung by a lovesick cowboy. The same buttons at Pinky's Pizza will bring forth rock and roll. Similarly, when the buttons of the mind are pushed, Othello plays "Your

Cheatin' Heart" and Hamlet sings "Did You Ever Have to Make Up Your Mind?" The push is the same; our samskaras dictate how we respond.

What we call personality is nothing more than the sum of our samskaras, the collection of our patterns of thinking. We are what our samskaras are; we see everything in life through our samskaras. Against the background of stress and illness this is a highly suggestive explanation, for it is samskaras that put us under stress and dictate our response to it. A resentful person goes through life under considerable stress, because he finds occasions for resentment everywhere.

The other day a teenage friend of mine gave me a pair of spectacles to try on. They looked quite ordinary, but they did strange things to what I saw. Everything was distorted and threatening. A friendly gesture looked like a karate attack; a smile seemed twisted into a grimace.

Imagine going through life with spectacles like these, which you could never take off. That is what samskaras can do. They are our patterns of thinking, and as we think, so we perceive. Most negative samskaras stem ultimately from insecurity, and where vision is shaped by insecurity, everything in life seems threatening. Different people may respond in different ways, develop different "samskaras of adaptation," but the result in all is stress – first in the mind, then finally throughout the body.

Body and mind, remember, are not separate. The samskara begins digging in the mind, but in time it sprawls over into the body too. It doesn't worry about permits or zoning; it just sends out its surveying crew to see where the ground is right for digging. Over the years, they test and test the soil. "Nope, not the lungs; those Alveoli are a pretty tight bunch. Stomach and Co. aren't too promising either. But this Cardiovascular family – ah! Signs of weakness. This heart's not too strong; let's work on his arteries." And the samskara starts digging, just where you are most vulnerable. It may be a more dramatic picture than Dr. Selye presents, but on the physical level, the action is much the same.

In one classical experiment in hypnosis, the subject is touched with a pencil tip and told that it is a lighted match. In a couple of minutes, a burn blister often forms. It is not that the mind has made this blister, where a "real" burn blister is made by the body. In both cases, the blister is made in body and mind together.

Interestingly enough, for this experiment to work, the subject has to have had prior experience of being burned. From that, the mind has an idea of what "burn" means. Afterwards, when it gets the message "You're getting burned," it reproduces the response it has learned.

The person with a strong negative samskara is similar. He feels threatened, responds in the same way again and again in his mind, and with each thought comes all the body chemistry with which it travels. Once the sequence is established, it can even be reversed. I knew a man whose jealousy of a particular person consistently brought on acute gastric distress. After some years, if he so much as ate something that disagreed with him, the feeling in his stomach would trigger jealousy in his mind!

But samskaras have a positive side too. Since they are a process, personality is a process also. Just as every tissue of the body is in a continuous state of repair, we are constantly shaping our personality by what we think, say, and do. As long as our samskaras are rigid, we have very little choice in this; we go on remaking the same old personality. But at a deeper level of consciousness, we can learn to go against these conditioned ways of thinking and actually change ourselves from the inside out.

This is a strenuous, painful, difficult challenge. The very meaning of the word "conditioning" is that the connections between thought and action have become automatic, out of our control. In this sense, the whole purpose of meditation is to extend the conscious will deep into the unconscious mind, beneath the level from which samskaras spring.

The underlying principle of this can be stated simply: we become what we meditate on. When you take a passage from the Sermon on the Mount or the Bhagavad Gita and go through it slowly in your mind with complete concentration, you are driving its ideals deep into consciousness. In effect, you are digging new samskaras – kind ways of thinking instead of resentful ones, patience instead of anger. Then, during the day, you draw on the power released in meditation to try to act on these new samskaras instead of on the old. Nothing is more difficult. When someone is rude to you, just try being kind in return; angry words will pile up behind your clenched teeth. But every time you succeed, you have dug your new samskara a little deeper. When they run deep enough, prana will flow naturally down these new channels instead of down the old – and a major part of your character, consciousness, and conduct will be transformed.

Even the nervous system seems to be reconditioned by this transformation. Where a destructive samskara like anger releases toxins and lowers resistance, a positive samskara like patience, forgiveness, or compassion protects and heals. Patience, for example, is the best health insurance I know. Patience is a dynamic quality; I am not talking about repression. A patient person is not usually subject to ulcer or high blood pressure, for the simple reason that he or she does not feel under stress. A patient mind is a calm mind, secure, unthreatened by life. Consequently, the immune system and the rest of the body become as strong as genetic limits will allow. For these reasons, I would go to the extent of saying that if a disease is not too far advanced, a change in one's ways of thinking at a deep level can reverse the course of illness or even bring remission.

Given the sheer impossibility of it, I always find it astonishing how swiftly the transformation of personality can proceed. It may have taken you thirty years to make yourself resentful, but in much less than thirty years you can become secure, loving, and resilient. The key is simple: how much do we *desire* to change? Patanjali, one of the foremost teachers of meditation in ancient India, tells us with deceptive understatement, "Progress comes swiftly for those who try their hardest." Whether it is tennis or transformation, the secret is the same: to achieve success, we need to master our desires.

Chapter Six
Will and Desire

DESIRE IS THE KEY to life, because desire is power. The deeper the desire, the more power it contains. The Upanishads say,

> You are what your deep, driving desire is. As your deep, driving desire is, so is your will. As your will is, so is your deed. As your deed is, so is your destiny.

Desire can be thought of as a river of prana, flowing along the channels made by samskaras. For the person with many small desires, prana trickles in many different directions. There is not much power in a trickle, and little desires often fail to reach their goal. But then, just because they are little, it does not matter much if many of them get nowhere. What matters is the sense of futility that builds up in a person whose desires are many and trivial. Like rain that falls on a mountain peak, running down the slopes on every side, vitality is dispersed; life itself is fragmented.

On the other hand, there are people whose lives are molded by one all-consuming desire, as overwhelming as a mighty river. If you have seen a great river like the Ganges or the Mississippi in flood, you know what power it can have; anything in its path is swept away. Similarly, the man or woman who has unified desires sweeps all obstacles aside.

Wherever you find great success in life, it is due to the intense unification of desires. Some years ago I read an interview with Margot Fonteyn, one of the greatest ballerinas in the world. When the interviewer commented on her effortless grace, she replied in effect, "It is effortless *now*. Behind the grace and spontaneity you see on the stage, there is the cruelty of the bullring." Years and years of grueling practice, day in and day out, starting perhaps at the age of ten. I don't know if you have seen a ballet teacher in action; what I have seen reminded me of a galley slave master, standing in front of these earnest, dedicated children lined up at the practice bar and saying all day, "All right, now, kick! One, two, three, four . . . "

Some of the best ballet schools, I understand, are as rigorous as boot camp. There are no vacations; you can't afford the lapses. No ice cream after school; you can't afford the extra pounds. And none of the other little pleasures that teenagers take for granted. Everything is ballet, ballet, ballet. That gives an idea of how deep young Margot Fonteyn's desire for excellence must have gone. It is not that she didn't miss having friends and vacations and ice cream; I am sure she did. But much more, she wanted to become a great ballerina. "You are what your deep, driving desire is": it shapes your will; it shapes your destiny.

I once had a physicist friend who thought all this talk about the power of desire was metaphorical. He would gladly discuss electric power, solar power, wind power, but harnessing the power of a passion or a craving – well, that was not dynamics; that was poetry. "Power," he told me sternly, "is the capacity to do work. Work is the energy required to move a definite mass a definite distance. No movement, no work. No work, no power."

My friend was a dyed-in-the-wool empiricist, whose life, so far as I had observed, was spent at his desk with his slide rule, his papers, and a perpetual pot of coffee. Day or night I had never seen him far from that pot, from which I concluded that just as power implied motion and work, physics implied coffee and inactivity.

Then late one evening I came out of a movie theater and saw my friend striding along like an athlete, several miles from his home. I was astonished. "What got you up from your desk?" I asked. "You're breaking the habits of a lifetime."

"Coffee," he muttered. "I ran out of coffee. I simply couldn't think about anything else."

That was what I had been waiting for. "Here," I said, "a very definite mass has been propelled two or three miles, simply by one little desire for a cup of coffee."

If there is that much power in a small desire, how much more must there be in an addiction, or in a powerful passion like sex? In a hospital I once watched for perhaps half an hour while a man in a wheelchair, his arms almost paralyzed, struggled to lift a cigarette up to his lips. It brought tears to my eyes to see what power that craving had. It stood over that man like a tyrant, demanding, "I don't care if you can't move your arm. Put that in your mouth and smoke!"

It is not always obvious, but we get in life what we deeply desire from it. If our lives are completed with some desires still unfulfilled, it is usually because we have cherished more desires than one lifetime could bring to fruition. Hindu and Buddhist mystics would go so far as to say that we have come into this life expressly to fulfill our unfulfilled desires, which as unconscious drives or samskaras shape everything we do. Childhood interests, likes and dislikes in school, choice of work, the person we marry, the way we raise our children – all are molded by these deep, driving desires.

This is particularly easy to see in a person of genius, for whom most personal desires are focused very early on one particular goal. When I look, for example, at the life of Albert Einstein, viewing it as one sweeping whole, it seems so clear how much was shaped by the deep desire to find one underlying explanation for the phenomena of nature. At first the desire, the samskara, gropes its way blindly but tenaciously, like an animal following a scent. It tries childhood thought-experiments about light, wonders about whether to go into mathematics or physics, chooses a job for the amount of time it will allow for "conscious brooding" about extra-curricular matters like the universe. Then, when it gets the scent, it pounces and pursues it heart and soul, often for the rest of life. "I soon learned," Einstein wrote, "to scent out the paths that led to the depths and to disregard everything else, all the many things that fill up the mind and divert it from the essential." Similarly young Alexander dreamed of conquering the world, Mozart of writing great music, little Thérèse of Lisieux of becoming a saint.

Somerset Maugham has illustrated this in a fine novel, *The Razor's Edge.* The title comes from the Katha Upanishad: "Sharp like the razor's edge, the sages say, is the path to Self-realization." The hero is a young American named Larry, who loses a friend on the battlefield and is plunged like Nachiketa into a search for the meaning of life. When the story opens, everyone's desires seem fresh, vague, almost incidental. As the years pass, each character moves with blind tenacity towards the fulfillment of his deepest desires: most of them self-centered, some self-destructive, all unaware that their desires were shaping their destiny. In the end Maugham realizes with surprise that without intending to, he has written a kind of success story. "For all the persons with whom I have been concerned got what they wanted: Elliott social eminence; Isabel an assured position; Gray a steady and lucrative job; Sophie death; and Larry happiness."

The ancient Greeks had a saying: "When the gods want to punish us, they grant us our desires." The Buddha would put it differently: we punish ourselves, just as we reward ourselves, by the fruits of our desires. For where our desires are, there our prana is also – our capacity to live, to love, to enjoy.

The Greeks illustrated this with the story of Midas, whose desire for wealth turns even his daughter into gold. The story may be myth, but it is none the less real. A deep money-making samskara conditions even our perception. Show a modern Midas a beautiful landscape and he will see a shopping center – and given the opportunity, he will turn it into a shopping center too. Just as in that experiment with hypnosis, where the idea of a burn creates a real blister on the skin, the shopping center is already there in Midas's mind, waiting to be turned into reality. He may achieve his desire and amass a fortune, but the same force that fulfills his desire brings also all the fruits of selfish craving: loneliness, alienation, broken relationships, the inability to love. It is of utmost importance, therefore, that we have some control over what we desire, and the key to desire is will.

"Will Quotient"

The power in desire is the power of the will. Every desire carries with it the will to bring that desire to fruition. "Strength," Mahatma Gandhi said, "does not come from physical capacity. It comes from an indomitable will." If the will is strong enough, anything can be accomplished; if the will is weak, very little. In my opinion, what counts most in life is not IQ but WQ, "Will Quotient." In every endeavor, it is the man or woman with an unbreakable will who excels.

Look at students, for example. I have been a teacher for many years, and I can testify that the difference between an outstanding student and an average one is often not a matter of intelligence but that the former has the capacity of will to come through in an hour of crisis. Even good students, for example, may put things off until the last minute, having a grand old time. But when the clock tolls the eleventh hour they are able to drop everything else and work far into the night, drinking cup after cup of coffee and finally turning in a good job. Because their job depends on it, or their scholarship, or their romance, instead of breaking down under the strain, they are able to fuse all their faculties through an act of will. When I had a student like this I used to say, "If only you could make this kind of concentrated effort part of your daily life, you would be a genius."

Most students I know, however, are not like this. They too postpone until the eleventh hour, with the same intention to make a big push at the end. "Why waste a good Saturday evening? Let's go down to the Café Mediterraneum and spend the night there. In the morning we can get up early, clear the desk, and hit the books for all we're worth." But while these fine words are being said, the will is sitting back in his corner and saying, "Not me! You can count me out." And sure enough, when morning comes, such people cannot get the covers off. They look at the pile of papers on their desk and do not know where to begin. After a while, they get dispirited. "What's the use? Maybe a little coffee will help me think better." And down they go to the Mediterraneum again. After that it is going to be even more difficult to get to work. When we procrastinate, we are using our will for a dart board: every time something is postponed, it stabs a hole in the will.

Many, many failures in daily life are no more than failures of the will. Whenever we become irritated, speak harshly, criticize, belittle, or vacillate, the will is lying down. The implication is surprising: even to be kind, we need a strong will. We do not necessarily mean to hurt people; we simply cannot control what we say and do.

Usually we excuse ourselves from this kind of behavior on rather flimsy grounds. Once I noticed a three-year-old friend looking at me with a peculiar glint in her eyes. "What's the matter, honey?" I asked.

"You'd better watch out," she warned. "I haven't had my nap."

That may be reasonable for a three-year-old, but a thirty-year-old has no reason to be ill-tempered because he or she got only six hours and thirty-seven minutes of sleep. The only reason we consider this a good excuse is that we are so physically oriented. When we begin to break through the conditioning of body-consciousness, we can be patient even if we go all night without sleep, simply because we have the will.

In daily living, a strong will often shows as a particular inner toughness, the endurance to put up with difficulties without breaking or giving up. Without this, we are at life's mercy. I have seen even great tycoons, men used to facing the bulls and bears of Wall Street with a will of iron, suddenly throw a tantrum because a line of traffic was moving too slowly. Where is that iron will then? It is almost as if they open their briefcases, take out a portable crib, climb in, and start to howl.

Here we can draw a surprising conclusion: a rigid personality is not strong; it is weak, because the will is fragile. In one compartment of life, where desires run deep, the will can operate; elsewhere it is paralyzed. On the other hand, those whose will is uniformly strong can always adapt; they can function beautifully no matter what life deals out. Such people are free. They enjoy life, ups *and* downs.

The Forest of Desires

The will does not grow weak simply through neglect. We attack it also, usually through absurd little self-indulgences: a bite of this, a drink of that, an unkind word, an unnecessary complaint. "What does it matter?" If nothing else, what matters is the will. Every time we give in to a self-indulgent impulse, we are twitting the will. The will can stand a lot of twitting, but after hundreds of twits every day for a couple of decades, it goes into hibernation. And not content with twitting, we often stage guerrilla raids: sneak down to the refrigerator, say, and drop a couple of extra items into our mouth. "After all," we ask, "who's the wiser?" No one may be the wiser, but the will is weaker.

Here the Buddha has a splendid image. Selfish desires, he says, grow in the mind like trees: first seedlings, so tiny you scarcely notice them, then a number of big trees, and finally a forest so dense that the branches and foliage shut out the light of the sun.

One of my friends with a consuming interest in reforestation roams the hills around his home planting seedlings, which he lovingly nurtures until just the right conditions are present. Once, I remember, a parcel arrived and my friend was delighted. "That's two hundred trees from the forestry service!" The box looked only big enough for three or four, but I looked in and there they were, not much bigger around than a pencil. Even after they were planted, it was difficult to take them seriously.

As the years passed, however, the seedlings began to look like little trees – one foot high, then two, then three. Now, after more than a decade, there are groves that shelter all kinds of wildlife. In a generation there will be whole forests, which people will say have been there forever.

All desires start like seedlings: unpretentious, harmless, scarcely to be taken seriously. At first, just a little thought: "That movie certainly seems to be popular. It's playing in every town." Then, "I wonder what made them rate it X." And then, "I think I'll just go see. If it's really bad, I can always close my eyes." The seed has germinated; the samskara has poked itself up into the level of behavior. And after a while – thinking about it, reading about it, talking about it, watching it – you get the desire to have that experience for yourself. Oddly enough, once this develops, circumstances seem to shape themselves in such a way that it is easy for the desire to be fulfilled. The place is right, the company amenable, and the next thing we know, our desire has outstripped our will. Little by little: first the seedlings, then a grove, then finally a full-fledged forest. Everybody with big, compulsive desires had them first as little desires.

Seedlings, as I said, scarcely seem a threat. Whenever you like, you can pull them up with ease. This is a stage that most of us recognize with desires. "I'll just have one cigarette after dinner. Uncle George smokes; I wouldn't want him to feel alone. After all, I can take 'em or let 'em alone." That is just the time to let them alone. It will strengthen the will only a little, but if you do *not* let them alone, you weaken the will considerably. Then, after a year or so, you may look around and find you are no longer ruler of a little grove of cravings; you are in the middle of a jungle.

When I was a Boy Scout in India, we used to play at tracking. One group would steal off to hide, leaving little clues as they went – a bent twig, a slightly torn leaf, one pebble on top of another. Then the other half would try to track down the first.

As long as we played tracking within our village, we were all right; nobody got lost. But once, I remember, our scoutmaster decided to treat us to a real adventure. Just north of my village was a huge, dense forest. This was not a play forest, like the ones where you ride down a miniature Amazon taking pictures of plastic hippopotami; this was real. When you saw a tiger, it was not stuffed. When you met an elephant, it was not a symbol of the Republican party. All this made our scoutmaster gravely aware of his responsibilities. "Obey my instructions completely, boys," he said, "and don't go beyond the boundaries. On the other side of that river, tiger cubs are playing tracking, and they like to track human boys."

A few of my friends, for whom danger was the sauce of life, had been waiting all through high school for a chance like this. They found some excuse or other for overstepping those boundaries, and after a while we realized that we did not know where we were. We got terrified, and the boys who were most terrified were those who had been most daring. We started hearing wild animals all over the place, and if our scoutmaster had not found us, someone else might have been writing this book.

Jesus says, "Lead us not into temptation." As things stand today, there is no need for any of us to go out of our way to cultivate our desires. They grow quite readily everywhere, and if we let them grow into a forest, we can get lost in the tangled paths of the unconscious, where wild samskaras – fears, anxieties, conflicts, compulsions – roam at will.

The Great Race

We can think of Will and Desire as competitors in a really long marathon, one that goes on for years. All the bets are on Desire. He has been training for many years, so he is in the best of shape. He crouches at the starting line like a leopard, lean, lithe, and powerful, bursting with the desire to win. But for most of us, the will is still in bed. I say "most of us" without any deprecation, for this is the conditioning the world shares today: the attitude that pleasure is everything, and the absence of pleasure the worst of fates.

Once we start questioning this attitude, a new desire comes: the desire to master our desires. That is the signal that the race is about to begin. But first we have to wake the will. "Willie! Willie! Your presence is expected at a particular event. Don't you hear the crowd roaring? Can't you hear the pom-pom girls?"

"Go away," Will says. He is as grumpy as a hibernating bear. After all, it is we who lulled him to sleep; is it fair to roust him out of bed again after all these years?

Finally we have to shake the will a little. Probably he will try to hit us. At that time there are people who say, "Who wants to be hit? Why not let sleeping wills lie?" They go back to watch the race between desires, in which no matter who wins, we lose. But the person with determination, who is tired of losing in life, goes to the kitchen, gets a pitcher of cold water, and pours it on Willie's head.

Will gets up fast, shaking off the cobwebs. "How about a drink?" We give him some black coffee. As he wakes up, he starts to complain: "I haven't run in years; I'm a marshmallow! Besides, I don't have any running shoes; I don't have any shorts. You wouldn't want me to run in my pajamas, would you?" We have to humor him: get the right apparel, tie his shoes for him, practically carry him to the race. Even then all the spectators look at poor Will and laugh. "He shouldn't even be here!" And in fact, he scarcely is — yet.

Will slouches at the starting line, all out of shape, while leopard Desire crouches eagerly. Many races have one or two false starts, where everyone has to come back and start again. Here the will is allowed a number of false reverses. "This is too much for me. I'm not meant for competition. You fellows go ahead and race each other; I'm going back to bed." He may even try to tiptoe off the track, and we have to keep bringing him back. The will needs constant encouragement, especially at the outset. We have to console him for being so out of condition, reassure him not to be self-conscious about the bulge about his waist, tell him the story of the tortoise and the hare — whatever it takes to keep him in the race.

Off goes the gun; Desire springs from the starting blocks. But Will is all engrossed in his feet. "Look, I've got my shoes on the wrong feet! How did that happen?" He bends over to untie them, and our hearts sink. "Willie, the race has started! Your competitor is already half a mile down the track."

Will lumbers to his feet to the jeers of the crowd. "Hey, Willie, don't go too fast!" "You shouldn't be on a track; you should have stayed in bed!" The voices are our own. There is a certain amount of self-deprecation when we try to master strong desires, but on no account do we need to take this kind of jeering seriously. Even if he appears weak, we should put our money on the will. The miracle is that even the Most Flaccid Will in the *Guinness Book of World Records* can be made immeasurably strong. Just as there are exercises for strengthening different parts of the body, there is a powerful exercise for strengthening the will – resisting any conditioned, self-centered desire. It may be for some sensory pleasure, or it may be more subtle: the demand to have our own way, to have others conform to our expectations. Whatever it is, if we yield to that desire, the will is weakened; if we resist, the will is strengthened.

This kind of training has to be practiced with artistry and a sense of proportion. I do not belong to the school of thought that maintains, "If it's unpleasant, it must be good for you." Not at all. I would not, for example, suggest you deprive yourself of a glass of fresh orange juice in the morning just because you desire it. There are plenty of positive opportunities for strengthening the will, by resisting urges that benefit nobody.

You can start first thing in the morning, when it is unutterably pleasant to huddle under warm blankets and doze. Do not stop to think; just throw off the blankets and jump out of bed for meditation. That wakes the will up fast. Isn't there a saying, "He who hesitates is lost"? I would not go to that extent; but hesitation, like procrastination, saps the will. Jesus often says, "Forthwith": do it now.

As Yama points out, preya and shreya approach us throughout the day. The more we look, the more choices we will find, many of them quite unsuspected. Being kind, staying patient, not making a clever remark at someone else's expense – all these strengthen the will. Go to work a little early, and leave your work in the office when you come home; it will strengthen the will. And if you can give your best to people around you and try to work out differences harmoniously, you are not only making the will stronger, you have him out on the track jogging.

In all fairness, I must say that the will is a plucky fellow at heart. After just a little training he is ready to compete, even if Desire has run so far ahead that he thinks he is unchallenged. And once he starts training, be it ever so slowly, the will gains ground every day. Finally Desire looks casually over his shoulder and rubs his eyes in disbelief. There is Will, rounding a far corner. He is not puffing along any more; he is lean, fit, beginning to feel his stride. Soon Desire can hear his footsteps, almost feel him breathing down his neck. At this point, I must warn frankly, Desire may start running for all he is worth.

But finally comes one of the most thrilling moments in spiritual development. This first-rate professional, Desire, suddenly finds himself running neck and neck with the amateur Will. For a while, in fact, we never know who is going to win; just a couple of inches can make the difference between victory and defeat. It makes us vigilant every minute, which is a prerequisite of spiritual progress. If we thought the race was in the bag, effort would slacken; growth would cease.

And at last the will gives one great leap forward, pulls into a strong lead, and breasts the tape. After that, your will is unbreakable. What may be called "right desires" – desires that benefit all, including yourself – can be as strong as they like; when the will runs ahead of desires, nothing can become an obsession. If a desire starts to get a little stronger, the will simply lengthens its stride and pulls out in front.

The Transformation of Desire

Desire and Will are close relations. They even have the same surname, Prana. One consequence of this is very practical: every desire draws vitality away from the will. If that desire can be resisted, the power caught up in it begins to flow into our hands.

Interestingly enough, when it comes to something we like, we have all the will we need. This is a terribly important clue. Someone says, "Hey, come on, we're going skiing!" and that is enough. We will get out of bed at three in the morning, drive for hours, stand cheerfully in the snow waiting for the ski lift, and in general suffer all kinds of discomfort with a will of iron. Yet as small a challenge as a letter to Aunt Gertrude will find the will against us; it will actually push us away.

In this sense, no one can plead that he or she lacks will. There is will in every desire. If the desire is self-centered or conditioned, our will is turned against us; we do what it commands. As Spinoza observed, in such a life there are no decisions, only desires. But when the will is in our hands, we control our destiny.

The Bhagavad Gita sums it up concisely: "The will is our only enemy; the will is our only friend." In Western mysticism, this enemy will is called self-will: the fierce compulsion to please ourselves, get what we want, have our own way, even if it is at the expense of others. This is the immense power behind all selfish desires. In deep meditation we can see self-will flowing through personality like a powerful river, conditioning most of what we think, say, and do.

Sometimes in spiritual circles you will find invectives against desire. I have even heard the Buddha misquoted as saying that desire is suffering. Not at all. *Selfish* desire is suffering – in fact, the source of all suffering. But desire itself is simply power, neither good nor bad. Without the tremendous power of desire, there can be no progress on the spiritual path; there can be no progress anywhere. The whole secret of spiritual transformation is turning selfish desire into selfless desire, transforming personal passions into the overwhelming desire to attain life's highest goal.

In my earlier days, I must confess, I would have agreed with the rest of the world that it is not possible to defy a strong desire without suffering serious consequences. When the river of conditioning came down on me, I too believed that I had no choice except to let the current sweep me away. But as my meditation deepened, I began to suspect that there *was* a choice. Instead of turning my back, I could turn against the current and try to swim upstream.

For a long time I did not succeed; the muscles of my will were not yet strong enough. But I went to work on strengthening my will, by resisting all sorts of little, self-centered desires. And gradually a wonderful thing happened. It was like recalling some old strokes I had once learned but long since forgotten – butterfly, breaststroke, Australian crawl. I said to myself with some amazement, "Hey, I can do this! I'm not being swept back any more." It gave me a whole new perspective. Instead of deprivation, going against desires became a challenge, a new sport. Just as there are people who like nothing more than to ride a turbulent, treacherous river downstream, I began to find a fierce joy in fighting my way against the stream of my conditioning, like a salmon returning to its source.

This is not repression; it is transformation. When I approved of a desire, I still knew how to swim with the current and enjoy it. But when I disapproved, I had a choice. I no longer lived in the everyday world of stimulus and response; I lived in a world of freedom.

In this sense, we can look on the will as a tremendous transformer. The tributaries of desire and self-will flow in; then out comes prana, to be utilized as you choose. If the will is unified from top to bottom, the moment anger rises you can transform it into compassion. The moment disloyalty arises, you can transform it into love. Every negative samskara can be transformed like this, which means that personality can be remade completely in the image of your highest ideal.

Ruysbroeck, a Flemish mystic of the fourteenth century, wrote, "The measure of your holiness is proportionate to the goodness of your will." As he told some university students, "You are as holy as you want to be." And, I would add, as happy as we want to be, as loving, as wise. The choice is wholly ours.

Chapter Seven

Clear Seeing

YA M A is a precise teacher. If someone tries to talk to him about the mind, he objects, "What part of the mind do you mean?" To describe this internal instrument of consciousness accurately, we have to distinguish between two components. One, sometimes called the "lower mind," is the domain of senses, emotions, and sensory desires. When we talk about the mind, this is what most of us mean. But there is another component, the "higher mind," which has no adequate English name. Sanskrit calls it *buddhi,* and it corresponds roughly to what we might call the discriminating intellect or judgment. Its job is to see clearly: to take a long view and see the whole rather than just a part, so as to distinguish between preya and shreya. But to do this, desire and judgment – the lower mind and the higher – have to work together as a team.

Responsibility for making wise choices, then, extends through many levels of personality. In this sense, the discoveries of meditation are a little like an extensive grand jury inquiry, conducted over a number of years as our awareness deepens.

First to be called is the body. He is the only corporeal party involved, so everyone suspects him first. But once we hear his testimony, he wins our sympathy. "I'm not to blame! All these years I've been getting demanding desires from the mind: 'Do this! Eat that!' Then when I get fat, they get a dentist to wire my jaws. If they want to wire somebody, they ought to wire the mind."

The mind confesses readily, almost smugly. "I am the culprit," he agrees, "and let me say, it took a lot of demanding to get this body conditioned. But here's the aider and abettor: undiscriminating judgment. Just look at this disreputable judgment, ladies and gentlemen, always mistaking the pleasant for the good and the temporary for the permanent."

So we confront the discriminating intellect. "Bud, you know the mind can't think for itself; it looks to you for guidance. Why have you been telling this fellow to eat whatever tastes good, to buy whatever Madison Avenue tells him to buy? Don't you know you have a choice?"

The intellect shrugs. "Sure, I know. But what can I do without the will?"

And the will, slouched in a corner, protests, "Don't drag me into this! We're not on speaking terms."

When will and intellect part company, it is not possible to see clearly. The will is like the muscles that focus the eye. When these muscles grow weak, usually through disuse, things at a distance appear blurry. Similarly, when the will becomes weak through years of giving in to personal whims and urges, we lose the capacity to see the whole of life or the long-term consequences of our actions. Don't we say that a person with poor judgment "can't see past the nose on his face"? When the will is weak, the attractions and promises of the immediate moment take up our whole field of vision, and judgment goes out the window. Then we can get caught in anything.

This process reminds me of the way in which elephants are

caught in India. A huge hole is dug in the forest and covered with bamboo matting and dirt, into which sticks of sugarcane are stuck in clumps. When the trap is complete, it looks like a little stand of sugarcane growing innocently in the woods.

Elephants cannot resist the call of sugarcane. The canes are tall, with bursts of bright green leaves, and the very sight of them seems to be so attractive that whatever thinking faculties they have are immediately arrested. All their self-control goes, and these majestic, slow-moving creatures start gamboling absurdly and kicking up their hind legs like lambs. There is a mad rush, the ground gives way, and they just tumble in. The awful part is that when one elephant sees those in front of him break through the matting, it does not even register in that huge cranium that the same thing is going to happen to him. The herd will stop only when there is no room left in the pit.

Most of us fall into infatuations in a very similar way. And the amazing thing is that no matter how many times we get caught, no matter how many times we see others caught, the next time is always going to be different. Like those elephants, we almost stand in line until there is room in the trap to try again.

Elephants, I should say, are strong, highly intelligent animals. Ordinarily it is difficult to hoodwink them. But like us, when a strong desire comes, all they see with those bright little eyes is the sugarcane. The trap, in other words, is more than just sugarcane; it is sugarcane plus desire. Suddenly the mind is asking only one question: "What will satisfy *me?*" When this question does not arise, our eyes are clear. We still see the sugarcane, but we also see the freshly dug ground and exclaim, "Aha! That's not the work of nature."

Once a friend of mine was telling me about a powerful adhesive that instantly bonds anything to anything else. "If you get some on your fingers," he warned me gruesomely, "you'd better not touch your eyelids! You'd have to call a surgeon to separate your hands from your eyes."

Selfish desire is that kind of glue. Over many years of close observation, I have come to the unfortunate conclusion that we can get caught like this in anything on earth – any occupation, any hobby, any habit; any fad, fashion, or philosophy, personal, social, or professional. We can be glued to opinions; we can be caught for a lifetime in the pursuit of a particular experience. And, tragically, we can be glued to other people, especially to those we wish to love. Whatever it is, once our eyes are glued, we go after what we want without even seeing the consequences.

Look at the effect this has on personal relationships, especially between man and woman. The moment we start asking "What can I get out of this," tragedy is inevitable. When Romeo sees Juliet, while his tongue is comparing her to "torches in the night" and "a snowy dove trooping with crows," his mind is quietly bringing out the glue. And Juliet is doing the same. The underlying state of mind is not at all poetic: "This is *mine*. Nobody else should have it. I must have it when I like, as I like, on my own terms."

Yama would not call such a relationship love; it is infatuation. There is turmoil when we are together and turmoil when we are apart: jealousy, manipulation, frustration, insecurity. We see things that are not there, exaggerate events beyond proportion, draw all kinds of unwarranted conclusions.

Interestingly enough, this is an almost universal weakness. Even someone with an IQ in the genius category, if he or she gets captivated by an attractive face, becomes like everybody else. The intellect closes its eyes, and we rush in.

At first, how sweet it seems! Juliet sweeps home in a cloud and tells her nurse ecstatically, "I'm really stuck on him!" But gluing has inevitable consequences, which are actually part of the desire. First come the pleasant consequences, and they *are* pleasant; no one would deny it. But afterwards, we are glued together for the painful consequences too. What stuck us to the pleasure now sticks us to the pain. A few months later, sometimes even a few weeks later, the very things that attracted us begin to irritate. What can happen next is something that harrows my heart. After a while, the same two people that professed their love now try to hurt each other. It is one of the saddest comments on compulsive desire: what we want is immediate pleasure; what we get is the glue.

In lighter moments, I have thought I might try my hand at a sequel to *Romeo and Juliet*. Instead of dying, the two lovers would get married and settle down together – long enough to become the noisiest couple in Verona. Once Juliet thrilled to the touch of Romeo's hand; now the same fingers feel clammy. Her lips seemed as unsullied as a rosebud in the morning dew; now he notices they are often in a pout. She was so innocent; how is it that she now seems immature? He used to be so witty; how could she have forgotten she detests puns? And their quarrels are all "Why didn't I stick with Rosaline?" and "I wish I'd never gone to that wretched ball!"

"Call it not love that changes," Juliet says. Very wise for a fourteen-year-old. Selfish attachment, infatuation, waxes and wanes; love only grows.

I have to confess that I am not a writer of tragedies. In my sequel, Juliet goes to her nurse and pleads – just as I have heard so many young people plead – "What happened to us? Is he different now? Am I different? Have I lost the capacity to love?" And the nurse tells her tenderly, "Not at all. Just get rid of that glue, my dear." When selfish desire is removed from a relationship, there is no hankering to get anything from the other person. We are free to give, which means we are free to love. Then we can give and support and strengthen without reservation.

Only then can we really see each other clearly. It is infatuation that is blind; love sees. The infatuated mind cannot help caricaturing. It sees only what it wants; then, when the desire passes, it sees only what it does not want. When two people are really in love, they do see each other's weaknesses; but they support each other in overcoming those weaknesses, so that each helps the other to grow.

Goals

Narrow, distorted vision is not confined to moments of infatuation. As long as the mind remains uncontrolled, this is our usual state. Only rarely is the mind calm and clear.

To explain this, it is helpful to say a little more about the "lower" and "higher" mind. In yoga psychology, the stuff of consciousness – *chitta* in Sanskrit – is described as a subtle, transparent, endlessly responsive medium. Just as if we were actually looking through it, the state that chitta is in affects how clearly we see, and how clearly we think as well.

When my wife and I lived in Oakland, we used to walk around Lake Merritt almost every day. Lake Merritt's usual appearance is an opaque brown, which I attributed to the color of the water itself. But one morning when not a breath of breeze was blowing, I saw an entirely different lake. The water was not brown or turbid; it was clear – so clear that I could see right into its depths and even read the slogans on the beer cans at the bottom.

That is the way consciousness should be. When chitta is calm, it is limpid and unruffled; we can see life clearly, with detachment. But every thought is a kind of wave in chitta, and strong desires constitute a regular storm. We rise on a wave of excitement, such as elation or anger; then, when the wave subsides, we fall into the trough.

Elation, for example, brings all kinds of grandiose visions. Today I saw a young man on the Berkeley campus playing his guitar under the trees. I needed only one look to see that for the moment, he believed he was the next Bob Dylan. Unfortunately, when that wave of elation falls, the same distortion of vision will be present, only then it will be negative. That very same fellow will be thinking that he is all thumbs.

These ups and downs go on much more frequently than we realize – ceasing, in fact, only in dreamless sleep. Even when we are not aware of them, they continue at a deep level in the unconscious, as anxieties, hopes, conflicts, and desires. As a result, chitta is in an almost continuous state of agitation, distorting perception and clouding judgment more or less in accord with our internal weather.

When we identify with these waves, life is full of turmoil. "I am elated," we say. "I am depressed." Actually it is not "I"; it is chitta, sometimes up, sometimes down. We are identifying with the lower mind, which cannot act; all it can do is react. Only the higher mind can stand apart from these storms. The application is completely practical. As long as we go on thinking "I am depressed, I am depressed," it is not possible to do anything about a depression. But once we can say "I am not depressed; my mind is," depression and other emotional problems become a matter of mental engineering. Waves have risen in consciousness, now they must be quietened; that is all.

The whole purpose of meditation is to keep waves in chitta from rising – not to suppress them, which can be dangerous, but to keep the lower mind calm so that the higher mind can see clearly. There is a close connection between this capacity and maturity. In an immature person, chitta is continually lashed into waves by the ups and downs of life around him. As we grow more mature, we identify increasingly with the higher mind, the inner observer that sits quietly watching and enjoying. When chitta is calm, the mind does not waver or vacillate; it is concentrated, observant, and secure.

To some extent, I can illustrate this from sports. If you watch the careers of champion athletes, you will find that those who stay at the top season after season usually possess not only skill and strength but self-control. They have some capacity to keep their minds calm in the excitement of the moment, so they can stand outside themselves and watch the most furious, fast-paced play with cool detachment, almost like those experienced pros who comment play by play for the television audience.

I saw an amazing example of this several years ago in a tennis match, when a teenage champion was pitted against a seasoned old-timer, Pancho Gonzales. At forty-six, having put on a certain amount of weight, Pancho had a dignified slowness about him which is not exactly an advantage on the courts. But he still had a strong desire to win, and he had won often enough to have some detachment too. When he stepped on the court, he was cool.

His opponent, on the other hand, was a big, bearded, wild-eyed European who was fairly throbbing for the play to begin. He had strength, youth, and a good deal of skill. I was certain Pancho was going to be beaten, and I felt a little sorry for him. Probably most of the spectators did also; you could hear "Pancho! Pancho! Olé Pancho!" resounding on every side.

Pancho took some time to size up his opponent, who was jumping about like a mustang. He himself was not able to move around much, but within a short while he had that mustang racing back and forth across the court, here, there, everywhere. Pancho just stood where he was, always one stroke ahead; the shots kept coming right to him. It was an amazing study in what detachment can do. And to the delight of the audience, Pancho took both sets.

By contrast, I had a cousin whose judgment used to vanish on the soccer field. As soon as the ball came to him, he would get so excited that he was likely to pass it to an opponent. Once he even scored a goal for the other side. After that, when he came out on the field, it was the opposing team who cheered. The rest of us would tell each other, "Don't worry about guarding *them*. Just keep an eye on Cousin Mandan!"

This is what can happen to the intellect. Without the will to keep chitta calm, the intellect gets so befuddled by the lower mind that it forgets the larger framework of its actions. All too often it ends up pursuing the wrong goals.

As a professor in India, I had always looked up to certain well-known authors, statesmen, and scientists whom the world lionized. But as my meditation deepened, I began to ask if they had made a beneficial contribution of their lives. Never mind if their work was brilliant; was the world a better place for their having lived? Objectivity often compelled a surprising conclusion. Many of the figures in my personal Hall of Fame climbed down from their pedestals and said with some embarrassment, "Let us out. There must have been some mistake; we don't really belong here." And a few came in shyly whom I had overlooked: men and women whose lives had been motivated by the desire to improve not their own lot in life, but the lot of others.

It is the purpose of the intellect to give us a detached view of life, against which we can assess our desires objectively. "What does this really accomplish? For whose benefit is it? At whose expense?"

Unfortunately, however, we seldom train the intellect for its purpose. We never teach it to give direction to our desires, or strengthen the will to be its ally. Instead we usually cultivate the intellect for its own sake, without any regard for consequences. We bring the intellect to graduate school and tell it, "Don't worry about what to study. Just bring your little chain saw every day and saw things up into subcategories for a few years." We get caught in what we like, and the intellect goes to work. Whether anybody benefits from that work does not even enter the picture.

If this sounds strong, please remember that the world of education is very dear to me. It is because I place a high value on what education can and should do to enable people to live wiser, richer, and more loving lives that I am so distressed by what it often does instead. Look at some of the subjects the well-educated intellect chooses to study for a dissertation. "Is There a Relationship Between Ambient Temperature and Dating Preference in Urban Teenagers?" I do not deny that subjects like this can be fascinating. But on the other hand, where is their pressing urgency? Ironically, their researchers will probably be invited all over the world to give lectures, even in countries where problems like violence or starvation cry out for attention from those who are intellectually trained or highly skilled.

Real "higher education" should develop the higher mind: teach us how to choose, how to master desires and strengthen the will, how to make the mind proof against insecurity and the body proof against the ailments of stress. Instead, as the president of a major university in this country remarked recently, young people still leave our colleges and universities essentially the same as they were when they first arrived from Battle Creek or Pinole – the will no stronger, vision no clearer, and no better idea of how to transform anger into compassion or hatred into love.

"From Death to Death"

To some extent, it is the nature of the intellect to narrow our vision and give it focus. Tragedy comes when we forget this limitation and think the intellect can comprehend things as a whole. The intellect views the world through a slit. When a cat walks by, it observes the eye, then fur, and then the tail, and then it infers that the eye is the *cause* of the tail – unless, of course, the cat was walking backward. If this sounds absurd, some of the theories about biochemistry and behavior use very similar reasoning.

Nachiketa would object, "Man, why don't you open the door? That's just your black cat Frodo, pacing back and forth." But instead we usually get caught up in classifying slit-information, even though without a larger view our conclusions may be entirely wrong. To make matters worse, we specialize. I am not against specialization per se, but what often happens is that we do not even look through a whole slit; we subdivide. My field is the upper part of the tail; yours is the lower. I might even forget about the eye and the fur. My main concern will be my debate with a colleague in Tokyo over whether hair on the tail grows up or down. If anybody asks how the eye fits in, I refer him to another researcher. After all, what have eyes got to do with geotropic hair growth?

Debates like this cannot be resolved on the slit level. What is required is to open the door; then argument becomes unnecessary. Once the door is opened, even a little, we will not quarrel over whose slit is correct or whether we should confine ourselves to the top of it or the bottom. As long as we see only part of the picture, logic and argumentation can never settle an issue. When the intellect becomes calm and clear, theory gives way to demonstration.

It is not beyond our reach to see life whole. We have simply become so attached to this precious slit that we think there is no higher mode of knowing. After a while, we become so used to slits that we put on a special mask with just a hairline crack in front of the eyes. Try walking around wearing a mask like this and see what happens. Every little thing will fill your field of vision. You want to put on your cuff links, but you cannot see the whole room; you cannot even see the whole of your bureau. When you finally spot one cuff link, you jump to the conclusion that your partner has lost the other one. In a short time there is a quarrel. Your friends will say, "Why spoil life just because you cannot see? Throw away that mask and see things whole."

This is not so much a criticism of the intellect as of the limitations, and especially the overbearing arrogance, of the intellect that has not been given a sense of direction. I would not call such an intellect wrong, simply immature. I have some preschool friends who have planted a little corn, sunflowers, carrots, and beans in a corner of our vegetable garden; now they are expert farmers. One of them prefers to be addressed as Farmer Cat. "This is my field," he announces without a trace of doubt. "I know all about it."

"Mr. Cat," I say, "you sound just like a professor I once knew, only his field was ancient Egyptian coins."

Farmer Cat is not one to be thrown by words. "My field is corn," he says after some reflection. "And beans. Corn and beans."

If he were a little older I would remind him gently, "Farmer Cat, you know only a corner of that field – a little strip maybe twelve feet long and two feet wide, in which you have planted a few dozen seeds. There is much more to the garden." But by that time Farmer Cat would be old enough to object, "Are you questioning my intellectual integrity?"

The intellect that sees only a small corner of life makes a very poor guide. We follow it like the blind led by the blind. I see this illustrated every day in the newspapers, at levels ranging from the personal to the global. To take just one urgent example, I have read that perhaps half a million scientists and engineers around the world are engaged in weapons research. I have no doubt that the vast majority of these people have no desire for war. They feel they are only doing a job, playing a small role in an inevitable activity. Nevertheless, this is not a "defense industry"; this is half a million highly skilled men and women preparing for war.

Producing and selling instruments of war is one of the biggest businesses in the world today. Even before the First World War, George Bernard Shaw caught the spirit of the industry in the character of Undershaft in *Major Barbara*. Undershaft is no sinister "merchant of death." He is just a businessman, whose credo is "to give arms to all who offer an honest price for them, without respect of persons or principles, to capitalist and socialist, to Protestant and Catholic, to burglar and policeman, to black man, white man, and yellow man, to all sorts and conditions, all nationalities and faiths, all follies, all causes, and all crimes."

Since Undershaft's time – the turn of the century – the world has scarcely seen peace for longer than two years, with the result that a run-of-the-mill arms salesman sells more today in twenty-four hours than Undershaft did in his whole life. Total military expenditures in 1990 were almost two and a half billion dollars of public funds every day – down somewhat since the collapse of the Soviet Union, but still a staggering amount, and double what it was when I wrote this book in 1981. In the thirty-some years since I came to this country in 1959, the amount that the world has spent on war and preparation for war is estimated at twenty-one *trillion* dollars. Yet the biggest market for arms remains the Third World, in developing nations where there are far from enough hospitals and schools, and often not even enough food.

The defense-minded intellect might object, "That's unfortunate, but defense is necessary. Everybody has to have weapons, and somebody is going to sell them. These have been good years for business, and here is a business that is thriving." There is no doubt that it is thriving, but at whose expense and for whose benefit? If a starving man knows his country is spending five times as much on importing weapons as on growing food, I doubt very much if it bolsters his security to see his leader standing and saluting while shiny new implements of war are paraded in review.

"These sales," the merchants argue, "help supply allies who cannot produce needed equipment." Needed for what? Any schoolboy knows that weapons are "needed" by people in order to kill each other, and it has to be admitted with some embarrassment that the "allies" we sell to have not infrequently used those weapons against either other allies or ourselves. From the evidence, we would have to conclude that death is a much more desirable goal than health, education, or welfare. After all, if two of your neighbors were quarreling outside, what would you think if someone ran up to sell each of them a gun? But no: the purpose of this profitable endeavor, as the best of intellects assure us, is actually to ensure peace.

Or look at cancer. Less than a hundred years ago relatively few people died from cancer; today it is second only to heart diseases as a leading cause of death in the United States. Many researchers today maintain that perhaps seventy to ninety percent of all human cancers are caused by environmental agents: chemical pollutants; things we consume, such as fat, tobacco smoke, and alcohol; toxic substances involved in manufacturing and processing new products. Most of these substances are relatively recent additions to our environment. We made them, and we can cease to make them if we choose. Yet one way or another – in their taste, their looks, their convenience – such substances, or the products they involve, appeal to us so much that life without them seems untenable. It is a very poor comment on our vision, almost like the story of the emperor's new clothes: the obvious solution is scarcely seen, and when seen it is deemed impossible. As a result, instead of trying to eliminate the causes of cancer, we pour millions of dollars into what one writer calls "the Vietnam of modern medicine": the search for a cancer *cure*.

This kind of myopia is not a necessary fault of the intellect. Given a larger picture, the intellect can rise to the occasion. Then, even if the Nobel prize is dangled before its eyes, it will refuse to work at any project that is at the expense of life, but will give all its attention to matters of real urgency. The fundamental questions in these problems are not intellectually overwhelming. If you were to tell an illiterate Paraguayan villager that the world cannot afford three billion dollars a year to keep its poor from starving, he would look at you pityingly as if you could not add two and two. "How about that two and a half billion dollars a *day* that you're spending on war?" If I tried to tell my mother, whose education got no farther than the second grade, that the incidence of lung cancer cannot be reduced because people *like* to smoke, she would wonder why I bothered to go to school. The choices are so clear; it is our fierce desire to do what we like that puts blinders on judgment and leads it round and round.

Here the King of Death uses his grimmest language. Blind to the consequences of his actions, unable to see anything outside her own narrow view, the man or woman with a clouded intellect "wanders on and on from death to death." This is meant against the vast backdrop of reincarnation, in which the individual personality is said to be reborn again and again until it learns to live in harmony with the rest of life. But Yama's words are equally true without reference to any other existence than the present. At a time in history when intellectual effort with a higher purpose could rescue a whole planet from disaster, we can almost measure the developments of our age as a grim march from death to death.

"Through a Glass Darkly"

From my school days I still remember some lines of poetry in my mother tongue:

> Flying high in the skies, the eagle sees
> All that happens on earth.
> Still, remember, even an eagle
> Can be caught in a net sometimes!

Our destiny as human beings is to soar high and see life whole. Instead, virtually all of us have been caught in the net of separateness. By what Einstein once called "a kind of optical delusion of consciousness," although we are part of the whole, we see ourselves as set apart from the rest of creation. Somehow "I" stops at my skin; beyond that is "everything else." And all my concern is with this little island "I."

"This delusion," Einstein continues, "is a kind of prison for us, restricting us to our personal desires and to affection for a few persons nearest to us. Our task must be to free ourselves from this prison by widening our circle of compassion to embrace all living creatures and the whole of creation in its beauty."

This is a good description of what happens in meditation.

Consciousness expands, and as it does, the mind clears. After many years of meditation, you almost feel you are riding in a glass-bottom boat, gazing into the depths of the mind below. You can watch thoughts arising long before they reach the surface of consciousness, while it is still possible to quieten or transform them. Not only that, when a wave of some powerful passion like anger or sexual desire is rising, hundreds of disturbing changes take place in the body as well as in the mind; all these can be observed. Most practically, when you contemplate a course of action, you see that action together with its consequences.

Whenever the mind becomes excited, we cannot consider the consequences of what we are about to do because we do not even see them. Actually, actions and consequences are inseparable, like an oak tree and the acorn from which it grew. When we perform an action, we are also performing its results. And as meditation deepens, even before you can see the consequences clearly, you can catch glimpses of them sharpening their claws and hear them getting ready: "Hey, old boy, put on your fangs!" It doesn't look so good. The intellect reports, "Do you see what you're letting yourself in for?" And you reply, "I think I won't do that after all."

Eventually, after strenuous practice of meditation and its allied disciplines, this delusion of separateness can be lifted from consciousness completely. When that is done, we no longer see only our own small corner of existence; we see life whole. As Saint Paul says, now we see only in part, "through a glass darkly," but then we shall see directly, "face to face."

Only then do we awaken to the everyday wonder of life. A seed is planted, it grows into a tree, and we are such hard-nosed men and women of the world that we cannot realize what a miracle it is. Every tree is a miracle, every bird. Imagine a huge bird like the heron actually rising into the air! We should cheer even if it gets as far as the post office, let alone if it flies to the Arctic Circle and back without so much as a compass. A few years ago I remember some close friends handing me their newborn son, so tiny you could tuck him into the crook of your arm. Now he talks, he walks, he throws things, he picks up his daddy's newspaper and studies it very seriously upside down. We forget what a miracle this is, simply because we lack the detachment to stand back a little from ourselves and see life whole. We skim the surface of life so lightly that we might as well be asleep. The man or woman whose mind is clear lives in perpetual wonder.

This is not just a matter of esthetics; it is vitally practical. After a hundred cases of some virulent flu, for example, even a conscientious doctor will often think, "Oh, here's just another case." That is not the patient's view. To him his case is unique, and so is his suffering. Every illness is unique in this sense; every death is a personal tragedy. When our eyes clear, if we read that thousands of children are dying because they do not have enough food to eat, those children are our children. We feel towards them exactly as we would towards our own flesh and blood. It releases the will and the resources to do everything possible to alleviate their suffering as long as the problem lasts.

"All creatures love life," the Buddha says. "All creatures fear death. Realizing this, do not kill or cause others to kill." The other day a woman I know, otherwise quite sensitive, was telling me about her new sealskin coat. "It's so warm and soft!" She had forgotten something that should always be vivid: sealskin coats come from baby seals, who would much prefer to be wearing their coats themselves.

"All creatures love life. All creatures fear death." Beneath the surface, the needs of all of us are very much the same. Yama puts it epigrammatically: "What is here is also there; what is there, also here." Whatever I need, you need too; whatever brings security to you brings security to me as well.

Our usual assumption is just the opposite. I get impatient over delays, but you are different; you don't mind waiting half an hour for me. I can't stand working with Ebenezer Scrooge – "What a disagreeable fellow!" – but while I grumble, Scrooge is probably sitting at home complaining about how difficult it is to work with me. The vast majority of human sensibilities are like this, common to all. No one likes to be the butt of a wisecrack. No one appreciates a condescending word, a cold shoulder, a curt reply. No one likes to be hurried, interrupted, or ignored. Similarly, whether we come from North Dakota or Timbuktu, all of us appreciate the "innumerable little acts of kindness" that express respect: listening with attention, remembering the other person's needs, not speaking harshly or jumping to unkind judgment.

And Yama repeats, "Those who do not know this wander on and on from death to death." These words are terrible in their accuracy, for all exploitation stems from this basic sense of separateness. "That person has different feelings from mine; he *likes* to be ignored." "That race has different values; they don't care about human life." Those who feel this way about other people, even about other creatures like the elephant and seal and whale, involve themselves and the world around them in an endless cycle of sorrow.

The French have a saying, perhaps from Voltaire: *"Tout comprendre, c'est tout pardonner."* To understand all is to forgive all. When we see the state of mind beneath behavior, we realize with great compassion that behind a sharp remark, an unkind glance, a rankling insult, an outburst of anger, lie a thousand contributing causes over which that person has very little control, extending back perhaps for many years. When a fellow has grown up in a little farming town, gone to Pioneer High School, spent two years in the Peace Corps, had such and so friends and such and so experiences, he is likely to get provoked by certain words and actions; that is what makes him who he is. Then the question is not "Why does he act like that?" but "Why did I not understand?"

Praise and blame are irrelevant here. You do not romanticize or close your eyes to defects or mistakes. You simply understand, which means that you do not judge. If a blind person knocks you off balance, do you get angry? If she fails to respond to the look on your face, do you call her insensitive? The vast majority of people are very much like that, blind to each other's needs. They do not mean to be unkind; they simply do not see. And instead of judging them or conniving at them, we learn to help them open their eyes. It not only enables them to change; we transform ourselves. "What is here is also there": in understanding ourselves, we understand others; in forgiving others, we forgive ourselves.

Chapter Eight

The Stream of Thought

EARLIER I DESCRIBED the mind as a field of forces, called samskaras. In equally contemporary terms, we can look on it also as a process – a flow of precise forms in chitta which we call thoughts.

When we watch this process for a while, what we see is the kind of meandering "stream of consciousness" that so fascinates some writers. If we could film our thoughts, in fact, I have no doubt that the result would win a prize in the experimental film festivals. We see a face; then comes some irritation, a memory, a grudge, a flash of anger, some unkind words, a desire, a hope, a twinge of fear, and so on, along a ceaseless course through past and future, among hopes, plans, remembrances, anxieties, and desires. When it is all over, the critics raise provocative questions: "What does it all mean? Why was that shot of Paris followed by those dogs? Why did we see the same memory three separate times?" Like a contemporary artist, we can reply honestly, "It means what it is." That is what most thinking amounts to.

In the deeper stages of meditation, however, we make an astonishing discovery: this "flow" is not continuous. Thoughts are formed, dissolved, and reformed in rapid succession; but between two successive thoughts there is no connection at all.

This has profound implications. For a thought-process to be compulsive, there has to be a connection between each thought and its neighbors; otherwise one thought could not cause the next to rise. When you begin to see that there is a little gap of no-thought between each two thoughts, all your responses can be free. At every moment there is a choice in what you think, and therefore in what you say and do.

This is an elusive idea, but I can draw out its applications with a number of illustrations. To do this effectively I shall be looking at the mind from several points of view. There may appear to be inconsistencies in this, as there can be if you try to superimpose photographs of the same object that have been taken from different angles with different lenses. But I am not trying to present a philosophical system. My sole purpose is to convey something that cannot easily be conveyed in words: how the mind works, so that we see how it can be changed.

In my village in India we used to celebrate certain holidays with fireworks displays, which were announced in a dramatic manner. We had a kind of miniature homemade cannon packed with gunpowder, and instead of a fuse the older boys in the village made a trail of gunpowder in little mounds, close to each other but not touching. Then the temple manager would ask for a volunteer – usually one of my cousins, the one who liked to play the part of a demon whenever we had a play. The priest would give him a torch. "Light the first pile," he would say, "and run for your life!" When the powder flares up, the blaze leaps to the second, then to the third. After half a dozen leaps the little cannon goes off with a roar and a cloud of black smoke, announcing to the village that the celebration is about to begin.

Much of our thinking is like that. Each little gunpowder pile of thought is separate, but each carries a kind of emotional charge. One thought or sense-perception comes, it reminds us of something else, and a little trail of explosive associations runs into the depths of consciousness and sets off a conditioned response.

Today, for example, I was watching people pass a bakery where all kinds of tantalizing goods were displayed. Most of them turned a little and paused to smell. Eyes to me are like little windows; when someone's attention flickered to a piece of German chocolate cake, it was like looking into consciousness where the mind was rubbing its hands together and saying, *"Ahhh!"* This is not cause and effect. The cake does not sit there outside us and tell the mind, "Now make some waves." The whole drama takes place within the mind. Chitta forms an impression of German chocolate cake; that is one thought. Then we think, "I *like* German chocolate!" That is a second thought. "I want some!" is a third. Not only can these three not touch, there is a little interval between them in which chitta is still – a little no-thought between thoughts. The idea that one thought causes the next is very much like the conclusion in the previous chapter that the eye of a cat is the cause of its tail.

Sometimes during those fireworks announcements, one of the piles in our powder trail would simply fizzle. We boys would run away holding our ears in anticipation and nothing would happen; we had to come back feeling a little foolish and try again. When you see each thought as separate, that is what you can do in meditation: take an explosive association – a particular memory, say – and defuse it of its emotional charge. With that one act, how many personal problems can fall away! The chain of conditioning is broken. You do not lose the capacity to respond; quite the contrary. But you no longer have to explode.

Another comparison is helpful here: a motion picture. A motion picture is more than just a few reels of film. It is essentially the process of projecting that film, so that what we "see" on the screen is continuous action. Actually, of course, what registers on the eyes is nothing of the kind. A picture is flashed, the eye perceives it; then the eye perceives an equal span of darkness before the next picture is flashed, and so on. Only when the projection is slowed down can we see separate images, and only when we stop the projector and look at the film do we see that there is no connection between frames. The whole illusion of motion depends on the speed of projection. Similarly, the whole force of cause and effect in thinking comes from the rush of the mind.

Meher Baba, an Indian mystic of this century, said succinctly that a mind that is fast is sick; a mind that is slow is sound. The diagnosis is quite accurate. "Fast," in fact, means a mind with many thoughts; the more thoughts trying to crowd through, the faster the flow. One thought comes and almost before it passes, up comes another hanging on to its heels. They rush past in such a tumble that we cannot separate or control them, and the result is the illusion of a continuous force. A stimulus comes and before we know it, up comes the response. The fast mind misunderstands, exaggerates, overlooks, and vacillates, rushing to judgment and jumping to conclusions.

The whole process reminds me of a game that children in India play called Monkey's Tail. Each child is a monkey. One little monkey catches on to another monkey's tail, a third catches the tail of the second, and so on, until you have ten or twelve monkeys all hanging on to the leader and running all over the place. That is thinking. A thought does not even have a tail; that is the comedy of it. And what happens in meditation is that each individual thought begins to feel a little silly. "I must be getting terribly shortsighted," it says. "Look at that! There is no tail at all." Then when you start to get angry, you feel absurd; where is the connection?

Fear is like this too, as I can illustrate with a vivid memory from my childhood. I had cut my leg when I was swimming, so my granny took me to the doctor in the neighboring town. He was a good friend of hers, so she managed to convey to him tactfully that I had a real aversion to pain. "Of course," he promised kindly. "I'll be as careful as I can. I just need to clean this up a bit and then apply some iodine."

Now, iodine is applied in India on the slightest provocation, and its acute burning sensation was all too familiar to us boys. So the moment I heard the word "iodine," my mind began to race and my heart fell into my sandals. I closed my eyes, and when I felt the liquid flow over the open cut, the burning was so terrible I lifted the roof off.

After a few minutes, everything subsided. I opened my eyes. "Was it dreadfully painful?" the doctor asked.

"Oh, yes."

"I haven't applied the iodine yet."

That is what conditioned thinking can do. It shows the remarkable power of the mind; one little suggestion and it creates a whole experience. The flow of thoughts depends surprisingly little on what goes on outside us. And the implication is marvelous: we do not need to change our environment to solve personal problems; all we have to do is master our thinking process and change our response to the environment.

Acting and Reacting

When I compare the process of thinking to a movie, people sometimes ask, "Does this mean that thinking is not 'real'? Is the connection between stimulus and response just an illusion, like the motion we see in a film?" The answer is in one sense yes, in another no. When the rush of the mind has been greatly slowed down through the practice of meditation, we can actually observe that there is no connection between stimulus and response. At that level of consciousness we also have the will required to translate this awareness into action, by ceasing to do what a compulsive samskara demands. With a lot of systematic effort, that compulsive connection can be cut once and for all. Only then can we say it was never "real." As long as the mind is flowing fast and these compulsions are acted on, the force behind them is very real indeed.

To cut these connections, we need to learn to slow down the rushing, unruly process that is the mind. Here again, let me use film as an illustration. The other day I saw a travelogue in which the main principle seemed to be "No shot longer than a second." The instant I recognized what was on the screen, something new was flashed in its place. It kept my mind continually grasping. After a few minutes it was too painful to watch, because this sort of thing is very hard on attention.

The fast mind is very similar to that film. It whirs along the same sequence of thoughts for a few frames, but at every suggestive opportunity it keeps trying to splice in extra footage. In cartoons, you know, you see a line and then suddenly it starts to bend, grows ears and a fluffy tail, and turns into a rabbit before your eyes. The same thing can happen when we think of a German chocolate cake. It is not simply a lifeless image; it becomes animated with tantalizing flavors – sugar, chocolate, and lots of butter – and memories. You remember the last time you had German chocolate cake; you remember the first time; you remember whom you were with and what you did. When this happens, you are really in another place and another time – a place not in the real world, and a time that does not exist. You settle down in a little corner to enjoy that cake all by yourself, and as far as thinking is concerned, you actually are eating it. There may be no calories involved, but your desires are inflated. A few more fantasies like this and you may find yourself in your favorite bakery, taking away a large pink box.

The vast majority of our thoughts consist of this kind of unnecessary footage. The more thoughts we try to squeeze in, the faster the mind has to whir along. The fast mind cannot even decide what to think. It has a lot to fit in, so it keeps cutting and splicing – first this desire, then that, then this again. When we believe we are doing or thinking two things at a time, we are really making the mind switch back and forth a thousand times, in and out of a lot of chopped-up footage. The results are painful: a divided will, poor attention, vacillation, and a great many other problems.

There are two basic tools for mastering the thinking process. The first is meditation, which is described in the Hindu scriptures with a beautifully precise image: there should be a smooth, unbroken flow of attention on a single subject, like the flow of oil poured from one vessel to another. In my own method, I make the mind go slowly through the words of a particular passage from the scriptures or the great mystics – say, the Sermon on the Mount or the Bhagavad Gita – as slowly as I can. Whenever the mind wants to slip off on another line of thought, I keep my attention on the words of the passage. It may take years, but eventually thought flows smoothly without interruption. Then attention becomes as powerful as a laser; it does not flicker, but penetrates to the core of a subject wherever it is turned.

The other tool is what in Sanskrit is called the mantram – a short, powerful spiritual formula that represents the highest we can conceive. Most major religious traditions have a mantram; some have more than one. Christians often use the name of Jesus or the Jesus Prayer; Jews, *Barukh attah Adonai* or the Hasidic formula *Ribono shel olam;* Muslims, *Allah, Allah* or the *Bismillah;* Buddhists, often *Om mani padme hum.* Hindus have a great number of mantrams, but one of the best loved is the one that Mahatma Gandhi used, *Rama, Rama.* Whatever it is, the mantram is repeated in the mind as often as possible throughout the day. Once it "takes," the mantram can become like a sword; you just repeat it a few times and the nexus between stimulus and response is cut. When your mind is stuck in some thought you do not like, you can repeat the mantram, lift your mind out of its rut, and switch it over to something better. Meditation slows the thinking process down; the mantram keeps it from acting on its conditioning and speeding up again during the day.

When the thought-process is mastered, the benefit is simple: you can think what you want, and you can stop thinking what you do not want. I have to confess that I did not appreciate the significance of this until I experienced it. When I felt exasperated or angry, it occurred to me that instead of dwelling on negative feelings, I might be able to draw on my meditation to do something about them. Then I made what was probably my most significant discovery in getting to know the mind. Whatever state the mind is in – resentment, fear, frustration, depression – if you learn to meditate, you do not have to dwell on provocations or bring up childhood episodes. All you have to do is sit down for an hour or so, reach into the depths of consciousness where the mind is whirring away, and cut off that negative line of thinking at its source. When you get up from meditation, the burden of those feelings will have fallen from your shoulders.

It is not enough to do this in the mind, however. Until we actually translate it into daily living, we are still living automatically.

My grandmother had a way of reminding me of this long before I was old enough to understand it. Every day after school she used to ask me what I had done. Once I replied, "I really lived it up today, granny!" I recounted all the activities I had indulged in that day, but she remained unimpressed. When I had finished my catalog she said simply, "You've done a lot of things today, son, but I wouldn't call them living."

It stung, but over the years I began to see that she was right. I was not living; in fact, I had very little say in what I did. My life was being lived not by me but by everybody around me – Tom, Dick, and Harry. I didn't choose to be happy; Tom made me happy. I didn't choose to get depressed; Harry made me depressed. They acted; I reacted. A good deal of what I did and even thought was dependent on how they behaved.

Once I took to meditation, I began to catch glimpses of what was going on in the mind. Samskaras were rehearsing a show over which I had no control. Even if I didn't want to act in a particular way, my samskaras would push me into action the way a bully on the beach pushes a small boy into the waves. It really made me angry. I wanted to say, "Who do you think you are, telling me what to do?" They played innocent: "We're *you*." But my understanding went deeper by then. Even if Dr. Pavlov himself had tried to tell me I was no more than my conditioning, I knew it was not true. More than that, I was prepared to fight to prove it. Once I understood that I was not even living my own life, there arose a tremendous desire to be free.

I wish I could convey how much energy I saved and how much security I gained when I began detaching my responses from what was going on around me. Without realizing it, I had always gone about wondering, "What is Tom going to say? What will Harry think if I do this?" But once I saw there was no connection between their thinking and my response, I began to concentrate on my own behavior. Whatever someone said or did, I tried never to speak harshly or discourteously. Partly I had learned that lack of courtesy never helps communication; partly I just did not like the idea of being a human jukebox, where someone puts in a nickel and out come a lot of unpleasant words.

I wonder if any place offers more opportunities to practice this than a large university. Wherever you are – at department meetings, in the faculty room, on the academic council, at a professional conference – there will always be some obliging colleague to contradict your opinions with pleasure and zeal. There is nothing wrong with this. Opinions clash easily when people feel concern, and in my opinion it is much better to have differences and clash over them than not to be concerned at all. But now I began to understand that it is possible to express strong convictions and face opposition with equanimity, without going on the defensive or losing respect.

As I learned to observe the flow of thoughts, I began to see that the whole drama of disagreement takes place within the mind. When I differed with a colleague, my quarrel was not really with him or his opinions but with my idea of him, my idea of his opinions. In other words, my thoughts were at odds with each other. There was my idea of what he meant, and then my response to that idea: "I don't like it!" The mind was flickering back and forth, which meant that I was divided against myself. And the application I found marvelous. If we have a problem in a particular relationship, no amount of external manipulation can solve that problem. The place to solve it is within the mind. When the thinking process is mastered, most problems in personal relationships can be solved.

In putting this into practice, I made a number of discoveries about the workings of the mind. One was that to learn to live in freedom, it is a great help to act the part. This gradually brings a measure of detachment. After all, when I got exasperated with a colleague, I was really acting a part I had not chosen. Why not change the script?

A few years ago I saw a film in which a skillful actor played the part of a dissolute man-about-town. After a while I realized with surprise that the same man was also playing the shy, retiring college student who was his foil. When the climax came, he had to play both parts together. I couldn't help admiring the ease with which he was able to switch back and forth: one moment the very picture of an experienced, world-weary *bon vivant,* the next moment speaking just like a bookworm in that peculiar nasal tone that sometimes goes with too much erudition.

As my meditation deepened, I began to see that we can have that kind of mastery over all our roles – parent, child, wife or husband, teacher, carpenter, whatever. Immediately I began to practice my acting. When I went to a meeting of the academic senate, I did not go as Eknath Easwaran; I went as Sir Laurence Olivier playing Eknath Easwaran. The opinions were the same, expressed at least as well. But when someone stood up to tear my argument to pieces, I learned to sit back with studied calm, knit my brow in proper intellectual indignation, listen carefully, and then take a few minutes to couch my rebuttal in good Victorian English. It enabled me to listen with respect and to reply without rancor, and interestingly enough, I found myself making a better contribution. Not only that, I began to get good reviews from the critics. "You were rather effective this afternoon," a colleague would say. "Not a bad point about academic standards."

I do not want to give the impression that this was easy. I had plenty of provocation. There *are* people who are disagreeable, and the normal, natural human reaction is to stay away from them. But the normal, natural reaction is conditioned, and I wanted to live in freedom. So I began doing something that was just the opposite of natural: I started to move closer to people I did not like, or who did not like me. And instead of becoming upset or antagonistic when I was with them, I became as vigilant as if I were in a soccer match. If the other person was rude, I took an extra minute or two to repeat my mantram and find words that were courteous, kind, yet still to the point. And instead of avoiding that person, I went out of my way to sit next to him and listen to opinions that were poles apart from my own. In a really difficult relationship, I even looked for ways to share my leisure time with that person: go to a play, perhaps, or play a game of tennis.

I must admit that I never did succeed in winning some of these people over. That can be terribly frustrating, and I remember reproaching myself occasionally for wasting all those hours on a losing battle. Then I realized that the battle had *not* been lost. In fact, I should consider those people my best friends; because of them, I had made myself so secure that I could function in freedom everywhere.

About this time I made another pertinent discovery: liking and disliking itself is a samskara, a conditioned habit. Beneath all likes and dislikes is a basic compulsion of the mind to pass judgment on everything: "I like this, I don't like that." When this compulsion is rigid, it is rigid everywhere – with food, with philosophies, and especially with other people. If we can learn to detach response from stimulus in any strong like or dislike, the whole likes-and-dislikes samskara is weakened. As a result, all our relationships improve.

One of the most effective ways to apply this is with food. Taste, as Gandhi says, lies not in the palate but in the mind. We like what we learn to like, and as often as not, we like what is not particularly nutritious and dislike what is.

In Kerala, for example, we have a particular kind of mango that is eaten green, when it is acutely sour. There is nothing inherently pleasant about this sensation; in fact, a detached physiologist would probably call it painful. But everybody around you likes it, everybody does it, so you learn to like it too. And in the end, you cannot do without it. It is a complete perversion of taste: what is nourishing tastes bad, what burns tastes good. Not only that, to add to the tanginess, South Indians combine such mangoes with hot red pepper and salt. There is a particular enjoyment in the way the combination sets your teeth on edge. In addition, we children had a special sauce of our own: we usually removed the mangoes by stealth from someone else's tree.

After I had been meditating for some time, I began to see that this was not a habit from which my body benefited. I stopped eating those mangoes; and of course my taste buds immediately brought out their little protest signs and went on strike: "Unfair!" My family was not much help. Some of my girl cousins would bring out mango, red pepper, and salt, sit down in front of me, and say, "What a shame you've stopped eating green mangoes!" It took some time for me to realize the full significance of what I was doing. Not only had I freed myself from a compulsive liking for hot peppers; I had weakened a little the whole likes-and-dislikes samskara. As a result, all my other likes and dislikes were a little looser, even in my relationships.

This discovery gave me the motivation for juggling with likes and dislikes everywhere – in the food I ate, the jobs I did, even the books I read. I wouldn't do something simply because I did not like it; some things are not only disagreeable but pointless. But whenever I found something beneficial that I did not like, I learned to do it with gusto. Over the years, it gave me quite a reputation. Once a friend at the university asked, "How did you ever learn to get along with Professor So-and-so?" I answered mysteriously, "By giving up sour mangoes!"

The Mind and Karma

Until the nexus between thoughts is severed, everything we think, say, or do leaves a residue of conditioning in the mind. The slightest thought has consequences, as does the slightest act. Over the years it is the sum of all these consequences, large and small, that shapes our lives.

In Hindu and Buddhist thought, this idea is called the law of karma. *Karma* has become a common word today; you can read it in popular journals, see it in the names of commercial products, even read it on T-shirts. But I think few words have been more misunderstood. There is nothing exotic about karma and its workings; it is a relentlessly universal force that operates always, whether we believe in it or not.

Norman Cousins, one of the most thoughtful commentators on our times, reiterated the law of karma in contemporary terms when he wrote, "A human being fashions his consequences as surely as he fashions his goods or his dwelling. Nothing that he says, thinks, or does is without consequences. Just as there is no loss of basic energy in the universe, so no thought or action is without its effects, present or ultimate, seen or unseen, felt or unfelt." But no one can improve on the simple words of Jesus, so powerful and so direct: "As you sow, so shall you reap. With whatever measure you give, with the same measure it shall be given you."

Literally, *karma* means something that is done. An action is karma; the consequences of that action are also karma. If John hits Joe, that is "bad karma"; John has to reap the consequences in an equal measure. Sometimes Joe hits John back, which is what I sometimes call "cash karma": the debt is immediately repaid and the ledger is clear again. Or, sometime later, somebody else hits John. A lot of time has passed, the person is different, so we do not see any connection between how John treated Joe and how others treat John. But the connection is there. An act, says the Buddha, is like an arrow; once it is shot, it cannot be stopped until it strikes the target. If we could trace the consequences, we would see John's action affect many other people until an angry Bob hits John. That is how the vast majority of people who believe in karma understand its workings, and it is an accurate picture.

But there is much more to karma than this. It is not only overt acts like hitting someone that produce karma. Baldly put, the law of karma simply expresses the fact that every action contains its consequences. If we share in doing something, we share equally in its karma.

A decade or so ago, for example, many people were ignorant of the health hazards of smoking. Today no one can be ignorant, yet cigarette sales are still increasing, largely because of some reckless advertisements that flaunt the Surgeon General's warning every time they appear. The law of karma would say that the men and women who contribute to these sales will have to share in the results – not only in the profits, but in the karma as well. The intellect may have a catalog of rationalizations, but in the heart of every one of us there is a subtle auditor that observes all that we do, shakes his head, and comments, "Shabby, shabby! You're helping to spread cancer and lung disease, you know."

But karma is more than physical action. Words cause karma too. If John hits Joe, he can treat the bruise with ice; in a few days it will be healed. But if John says something cruel to Joe, that remark may fester in Joe's consciousness for a lifetime.

Most important, thoughts cause karma. Thoughts are not insubstantial. They are more "thingy" than material things are, for it is thoughts, not things, that make up our experience. Thoughts are the very source of karma, for from our thoughts flows everything: words, actions, desires, decisions, destiny.

When this is understood, it becomes clear that karma is not imposed by some cosmic Lawgiver outside us. The judge and jury are right within, and so is the executioner. When we feel guilty for something, the executioner is at work. Whenever we feel resentful, hostile, lonely, or depressed, that is the sentence being carried out.

Anger, for example, is its own karma. When I see one person getting angry with another, I cannot help thinking, "That is one thousandth of a heart attack." I feel compassion for the angry person too, not only for those on whom the anger is vented. But most important, even if it is not expressed, a mental state like anger produces karma in the thinking process itself. Every angry thought makes it a little easier to get angry the next time, and a little more likely. We develop an anger samskara, and after many repetitions that samskara begins to invade our speech and behavior. We already had a tendency to be hostile; now we are making ourselves more hostile. With every repetition, the thinking process itself is deteriorating. Unless the deterioration is reversed, that very process will impel us into situations where we reap the consequences of these negative states of mind.

This does not usually happen all at once. At first we are simply making ourselves more disagreeable; so people naturally become disagreeable in return. But as the samskara gets more pronounced, so do the responses of those around us. People expect us to be hostile, so they stay away; when we are around, they are always on their guard. You can see how natural it is, and how marvelously precise; people treat us as we treat them.

Finally, if all these consequences do not make an impression, the time comes when we meet someone very much like us – a kind of karmic double with identical samskaras. Isn't there a line in English poetry, "When Greeks joined Greeks, then was the tug of war"? I would say, when samskara meets samskara, *then* comes the tug of war. That is how the karma for our thinking is finally reaped.

I can give an even subtler example: selfish desire. Even if it is not acted on, every selfish desire generates unfavorable karma in the thinking process itself. When we dwell on a desire, for example, we are making a little wall around ourselves and saying in effect, "I want this particular pleasure *here,* where I can enjoy it all for myself. I don't want to share it with anybody else outside." Unfortunately, by walling pleasure in, we are also walling others out. "Far apart are preya and shreya," Yama says grimly. "The latter leads to Self-realization, but pleasure only makes a person more alienated and estranged." After some years, that wall can become a prison; that is its karma. All of us know people who can think of no one's feelings but their own; their later years are full of loneliness and estrangement.

Of course, there is a positive side to all this too. When we refrain from acting on a negative emotion or selfish desires, that too generates karma – good karma. Again, there is no need for any reward from outside. The mind is healing itself, which is its own reward. We are more patient, so we suffer less from life. Our security is deeper, so we do not get shaken so easily by ups and downs. It is not only that life is happier; our very capacity for happiness deepens.

Karma comes back to us through our conditioning. The same samskara that impels us to commit a particular action also impels us into situations where we experience the consequences. The samskara sows the seed, and the samskara reaps the harvest. This is a terribly important point. If we can learn not to act on a samskara by severing the connection between stimulus and response, that particular chain of karma will no longer have a hold on us.

Let me give an illustration. Some time ago in San Francisco I saw a young woman on the corner handing out free cigarettes to passersby. People even crossed the street to get their little packet; some asked for two, muttering something about a friend. That is what greed can do.

Now, just to give an idea of how karma can work, I can sketch out a very simplified version of how the consequences of that job might take their course. This young woman, let us say, knew about the hazards of cigarette smoking, but this was an attractively easy way to make some extra money. After all, these were people who were going to smoke anyway; she was not making them do anything they would not otherwise do. So her desire for a little more money prevailed, and she took the job.

A few years later, she has a full-time job with a company that wants to promote her to a position in some industrial metropolis. And by now her money samskara has grown. She does not particularly want to move – the new city is dirty, the air is smoggy, her work environment would be competitive. But the salary is quite tempting. She takes the promotion and does well for many years, although the desire to succeed probably takes an increasing toll on her in stress.

That woman may never take to smoking; she may never even try a cigarette. Thirty or forty years later, if she develops lung cancer, those free cigarettes will almost certainly be forgotten. Yet according to the law of karma, the connection is there. This does not contradict the physicians who attribute her illness to a smoggy, toxic environment or a weakened immune system. These are immediate physical causes in a vast, tangled web. But all the strands are tied together by that woman's ways of thinking. Through the years, the same samskara that led her to pass out cigarettes on the street later made her choose to live in a smog-ridden area and work under considerable stress – all to make a little money.

Fortunately, this path can be reversed. If that woman learns to say no to her samskara, how many decisions will be different! She will not take jobs that are at the expense of life or health, her own or anyone else's. Her relationships will be richer and more fulfilling, for her capacity to love will no longer be caught in money. Passing out those cigarettes will be a mistake she did not repeat, and the karma for it will probably be very light.

In this sense, every time a samskara prompts us to action is a precious opportunity. Without the chance to make difficult choices, our samskaras would go on working away in consciousness, making our emotional problems worse. But when we find ourselves in some situation where we always make the same mistake, if we can manage *not* to make that mistake, the chain of karma can be broken. If we face it squarely, that situation may not even recur.

When we are young, usually ignorant of the unity of life, we have a wide margin for making mistakes. But as we get into our twenties, we are expected to learn not to go on making the same mistakes; for with every repetition, the burden of karma accumulates.

In karma, tragically, the effect becomes the cause. We not only generate karma for ourselves, we pass it on. Most of us, I think, have a tendency to say, "My world is bounded by my skin. I stop there; beyond that is a whole other realm." Actually, every person is an extension of ourselves. Just as we are very careful about not hurting our own hands, we should be equally careful about not hurting our partner, our children, our co-workers, or anyone else. This is not simply ethics or philosophy. When I get angry with someone, I cannot say, "This is just between George and me." It is not. It is between me and George and his wife and their neighbors and co-workers and all the other people in their lives who will pass my anger along. "I am involved in mankind," John Donne wrote. We are all involved, through the web of karma.

In the later stages of meditation, we get glimpses of how vast this web is, how far it extends. Everything we do affects others, even everything we think. That is why it is so essential to learn to break the chain of cause and effect, so that we become not an instrument of others' karma but in the beautiful words of Saint Francis, an instrument of God's peace.

The Still Mind

Ultimately, karma is generated by the thinking process itself. Whatever our thoughts, as long as they flow, words and actions have to follow, just as a piece of machinery goes on running as long as it has a flow of electricity.

When I was growing up, our village did not have its own source of power. As one consequence, films were a rare event. Some enterprising fellow with a truck used to travel from village to village with a movie projector, a battered print of some Bombay hit, and a little gasoline generator, and show the film in the open air. Through half the night you could hear the *tut-tut-tut-tut* of the dynamo all over the village, so that without even seeing the screen, you knew the film was being shown. But afterwards everything was silent. The generator was not running, there was no power, so there was no appearance of action on the screen.

That is how it is with karma. The source of all karma is self-will, the deep, driving desire for personal satisfaction — if necessary, at the expense of others. As long as self-will is present, selfish desires have to flow. Desire means a flow of thoughts towards a particular goal: we want some thing, we want some person, we want to get our way. When this flow is hindered, all kinds of negative responses are produced: irritation, hostility, resentment, censure, anger. Similarly, as long as the desire lasts, there is a flood of thoughts about the future: worry, apprehension, hope, expectation, insecurity, the fear of loss or failure. "Will this desire be satisfied? Will that person behave the way I want? Will I get this when I want it, in the way that I expect?"

With impeccable accuracy, the Bhagavad Gita reduces all these kinds of thoughts to three: anger, fear, and selfish desire, all flowing from self-will. From these come all karma and all suffering.

As usual, the Buddha puts it succinctly: "When this arises, that arises; when this falls, that falls." The "this" is self-will, and "that" refers to a whole catalog of afflictions: alienation, delusion, infatuation, illness, death, and so on, almost like a biblical plague. Once we let self-will in, all the rest follow.

I like to imagine the Buddha asking his disciples, "Do you want to be sick?"

"No, Blessed One."

"Do you want to be lonely?"

"No, Blessed One."

"Do you want to be hostile, despairing, at the mercy of life's inevitable ups and downs?"

"Oh, no, Blessed One!"

"Then you must prevent self-will from rising." When the ego is silent, everything in the catalog disappears.

Then the mind is completely still. Every moment is complete unto itself. The movie projector of desires shuts down completely, and in place of its clatter, we experience the blissful, utter stillness called *shanti* in Sanskrit, "the peace that passeth understanding." This is not an unconscious state; it is fully wakeful. But self-will is absent, along with all it entails. We can still think, when we choose to. But if it serves no purpose, we simply let the mind rest. Most thoughts, after all, are not so terribly useful. Worry, for example – do we really need it? Resentment, anxiety, dwelling in the past or future, what purpose do they serve?

When the mind is still, we are lifted out of time into the eternal present. The body, of course, is still subject to the passage of time. But in a sense, the flickering of the mind is our internal clock. When the mind does not flicker, what is there to measure change? Time simply comes to a stop for us – or, more accurately, we live completely in the present moment. Past and future, after all, exist only in the mind. When the mind stops, there is no past or future. We cannot be resentful, we cannot be guilt-ridden, we cannot build future hopes and desires and fears on past experiences; no energy flows to past or future at all.

Past and future are both contained in every present moment. Whatever we are today is the result of what we have thought, spoken, and done in all the present moments before now – just as what we shall be tomorrow is the result of what we think, say, and do today. That is the real implication of the law of karma, and it puts the responsibility for both present and future squarely in our own hands.

Chapter Nine

Shadow and Self

WHEN WE HEAR TALK about stilling the mind, most of us get apprehensive; it sounds a little too much like putting our personality to sleep. When I took to meditation, friends used to protest with the best of intentions, "You have a good mind; why should you want to still it?" Americans often put it more vigorously: "Do you want to become a zombie?"

This sort of question arises only because we think we are the mind. The mind-process is as compelling as a suspenseful film; while it is going at full speed, we can be aware of nothing else. But when this process is stopped, we discover with surprise that there is not just one self in us; there are two.

In Sanskrit, these two selves are called *jiva* and *Purusha*. Jiva is the individual ego, the whole bundle of samskaras that we call our personality. To each of us, this bundle seems to be a perfectly substantial person – ourselves. Yama would point out drily that there is nothing substantial about it at all. Personality is a process, the flow of consciousness, never the same at any two moments. Yet we cling to it as if it were solid and everlasting. It is constantly changing, yet on this ever-shifting foundation we try to build our identity.

If jiva is the personality, Purusha is our real Self, simply another name for the Atman. The personality we are used to is only a mask worn by our real Self. If we find this difficult to believe, it is merely because we have worn this mask so many years that we do not even know it can be taken off, while our real face — "the face beneath all faces," Nicholas of Cusa calls it — we have never seen at all.

These two selves, jiva and Purusha, are like shadow and reality. A shadow does have reality, it must be admitted. But it comes and goes, and you can put your hand right through it; it is both there and not there. A physicist, in fact, would say that a shadow is only the absence of light. The implication is deadly: the personality with which we identify ourselves is no more than a shadow cast by the Self. Without exaggeration, it is the absence of personality. Just as a shadow is produced when light is blocked, the jiva is what we see when the light of the Self is obstructed by self-will. This is the grand illusion that Hindu mysticism calls *maya:* we take the shadow for reality, while our real Self, if we even guess at it, seems shadowy and unreal.

Oddly enough, we give all our attention to this shadow self. We give it fashionable clothes, decorate it with current opinions, and take it around to be introduced to all our friends. A couple of years ago, when I was walking with my wife in San Francisco's Union Square, a young mime artist walked by with her arm outstretched just as if a little dog were trotting along ahead of her, pulling on its leash. When her nonexistent pet started to run off somewhere else, she would whistle for it to come along. That is exactly what we do with the ego. The main difference is that as long as we believe in it, the ego can cause a lot of trouble. Until it is extinguished, the ego is very real indeed. I know several people who have read that the ego and its problems are unreal and then gone out and done whatever they liked, saying, "What does it matter?" It matters a good deal.

Only when we actually come face to face with the Self, shake its hand, and say "Pleased to meet me, how am I?" does the ego actually disappear. Until then, all our personal problems have to be resolved as if the ego were a bona fide member of the club.

The King of Death describes our two selves poetically but with incisive accuracy. *"Names:* Jiva and Purusha. *Residence:* 'the secret cave of the heart.' *Occupations:* taster and enjoyer. *Place of work:* the fountain of life."* Mr. Jiva, in other words, is an impression-taster. He samples experiences all day long and renders his opinion on each one: "I like this, I don't like that."

Interestingly enough, whether the drink is sweet or bitter, the ego can always swell. But what he flourishes on is pleasure. Pleasure is to the ego what ice cream is to a child. When something pleasant is coming his way, he will sit and feast his eyes on it for a long while before even digging in, the sight is so appealing. The very thought of satisfying a personal craving seems to make Mr. Jiva's day a little brighter, the sky a little more blue.

While Jiva rushes around drinking all he can from the fountain of life, completely embroiled in his likes and dislikes, the Self simply watches and enjoys. Ironically, Jiva cannot really enjoy anything, for the simple reason that he is too busy rushing around. The Self is the only detached observer who can sit back and say, "Yes, that's good."

I used to see this illustrated on the Berkeley campus, where the main entrance is crowded with food vendors. Students come along with the harassed look of someone late for class, grab a knish, and stuff it in their mouths without even stopping. There *is* a little satisfaction in it, I am sure. But on the other hand, they are not really aware of anything going in; they are too busy being late.

That is how Jiva goes through life. Even while he is tasting something, his thoughts are darting off somewhere else: remembering some better taste in the past, wondering how long the pleasure will last this time, planning what he will sample next; scarcely present here and now to enjoy or to be aware. William Blake says,

He who binds to himself a joy
Doth the winged life destroy.
But he who kisses the joy as it flies
Lives in eternity's sunrise.

As a result of all this constant sampling, Mr. Jiva gets obese. If we let him eat whatever he likes, he careens through life like those big mobile homes you see sometimes on the highway, with red flags sticking out at the sides and signs front and back: "Wide Load." No wonder so many of us cannot get close to each other without colliding!

Purusha, on the other hand, has an elusive set of dimensions: "Smaller than the smallest, greater than the greatest." As long as we go on feeding Jiva, the Self seems so small that we cannot even see it. Therefore, even if we are president of the corporation or get our picture on the cover of *Time,* we are small too. But fortunately, Jiva can be put on a reducing diet. As we free ourselves from the conditioning of our likes and dislikes, the ego gets slimmer and slimmer, just as if he were losing weight at Eileen Feather's. We can show pictures before and after. First Jiva is really huge, so bloated he can't even bend to touch his knees. But after the rather strenuous regimen prescribed by the King of Death, he begins to get compact and supple: he is not so rigid about his opinions, is able to bend gracefully when it benefits others, doesn't bump into people or crowd them out of his way. And finally he gets so slim he simply disappears like the Cheshire cat, leaving only his grin behind. Then we are Purusha, "greater than the greatest": no longer the self-centered, transient ego-process, but a powerful force from which all life benefits. This is the real meaning of the title which an adoring India gave to Mahatma Gandhi: *maha* means great, *Atman* is the Self.

To discover this Self, we have to take up a kind of inward spelunking and make our way into the "secret cave of the heart": the regions of the mind. I do not know if you have ever explored an earthly cave; the experience can be quite unsettling. Without exaggeration, it is a wholly other realm from the surface world you have left. Only a little way in, you find yourself in places where light has never penetrated. You have to carry a kind of miner's lantern with you, and the darkness is so deep and the light so feeble that it takes some time for your eyes to make out anything at all. As you go deeper, the pressure seems to mount, your eyes play tricks on you, your sense of direction fails.

Descending into the unconscious in meditation is very much the same. You are in dark new realms; at each level you have to learn afresh how to see and walk without stumbling. Only after some years does it become clear that you are actually walking into regions of increasing light. Then, as the Gita puts it, what the world calls day seems to you to be darkness – just as to the rest of the world, you seem to be living in the night.

It is a great irony that our real Self, which the Sufis say is nearer to us than the body is, should be hidden away quietly in a cave like this while the false self, the ego, proclaims himself on every billboard in consciousness. It makes life like a game of hide-and-seek, which the Hindu and Buddhist mystics say has been going on for many lives.

When I was growing up, my grandmother used to stand on the veranda and ask all the children in the family to line up in front of her and close their eyes. Then she would throw a tiny tamarind seed into the grass and ask us to find it, with nothing to go on but the sound. While we were groping for the seed, Granny would say, "Near . . . . near . . . very near!" And at last one of us would hold it up and exclaim, "I've got it!" It was a real exercise in concentration. Two or three girls among my cousins were very good at this game, and to this day I am not sure they did not peek.

Similarly, when we draw nearer to the Self, there are certain signs that are much like my granny's "near, near": our security improves, we find it easier to forgive, we do not dwell on ourselves. And as we move farther away, we become more irritable; we develop stomach problems, hypertension, loneliness, depression. An upsettable mind and chronic ailments are the Self's way of saying, "Farther . . . farther . . . very far. You're going the wrong way!"

One of the most painful aspects of moving farther from the Self is that we cannot understand what it is telling us. It sits in its cave calling, "Farther! Farther!" and we just say, "What?" Meanwhile the ego is sitting right up front yelling, "Nearer! Nearer! Nearer!" After all, he has a vested interest, and he is a first-rate ventriloquist. He can reproduce perfectly the tones of sympathy, of martyrdom, and especially of utter conviction. I have heard people tell me as they embarked on a wrong course, "I haven't the slightest doubt this is the best move for me."

The Tree of Life

According to Yama, the whole modern world has been laboring under this one colossal superstition – that we are not what we are, and are what we really are not. The issue is much more than philosophical, for this fatal fallacy has plundered the earth, polluted the environment, and sown discord all over the world, between individuals, within communities, among nations. It is no exaggeration to say that if civilization is to survive, this false idea of personality has to be abandoned. But more than that, if we are to live in security as individuals, we have to disidentify ourselves with this shadow image and learn to identify ourselves completely with the Self.

Yama explains this with a vivid image: the Tree of Life. You will not find this tree in Bailey's *Cyclopaedia*. Its branches, leaves, and so on are the phenomenal world: matter and energy, space and time, body and mind. This is the world of process, characterized by ceaseless change. But the taproot of the tree is Purusha itself – eternal, changeless, unbroken consciousness.

According to this conception, the cosmos developed out of Purusha very much the way a tree grows from a seed. There are precise stages in this development, from undifferentiated consciousness – the trunk – all the way to the outermost leaves, the senses. Philosophically this can get quite complicated. But the important point is that the taproot of all existence is the Self. It follows that the more sense-oriented we are, the farther we are going from the roots of our being; and the farther we go, the more separate we feel and the more alienated we become. Those who identify with sense-leaves are really out on a limb; any strong breeze can cut them off from their source of sustenance. They become easily insecure, easily frustrated; after a while they may find life so monotonous that it is not worth living.

In meditation, as we can verify for ourselves, we actually reverse this process and return to our source, the taproot of our being. Over a period of years we learn to withdraw consciousness from the sensory level into the mind, then into the intellect, and then into the pure sense of "I," in which only a shell of separateness remains. Finally, in the tremendous climax of meditation called *samadhi,* all separateness goes; we are back inside the seed, the Self, from which everything else has sprung. Afterwards we learn to make this great journey at will, until samadhi becomes permanent and continuous. This is a very satisfying state. No matter what we are doing, we are always in touch with the source of our being.

Take a botanist on a tour of an orchard and tell her, "These trees just stand here. The trunks must be glued to the soil." She would look at you as if you had lost your wits. "They've got to have roots."

"'Roots'? What are those? I don't believe in roots; I've never seen one."

"The least you could do is dig into the soil and look!"

It is not a matter of blind faith to believe that there is a taproot for existence; it is simply a matter of spiritual horticulture. If we care to we can get a trowel, dig into consciousness, and find out for ourselves.

Let me take this a step further. Suppose someone looks at a pine tree and says, "This is not one organism; it is thirty-five separate branches. Talking about 'trees' is improper; we should speak only of independent branches and thousands of separate needles." Who would take such an idea seriously? But we do just that when we talk about the family of living creatures. As long as our attention is focused on the physical level of consciousness, all of us can be trapped in the assumption that the vast cosmos, the myriad processes of life, and the realms within the mind have simply evolved, with no real purpose, no common ground, no unity.

In fact, all of life springs from the same root. The Self in each of us is one and the same. For this Self, different names are given in different traditions. Christian mystics call it the Christ within. When a person ceases to identify with his perishable self, they say he has become Christ-conscious. Saint Paul says, "I was dead, and yet I live: yet not I, but Christ liveth in me." Saint Catherine of Siena says daringly, "My I is Christ, nor do I recognize any other I than He." In the same way, Hindu mystics often speak of Krishna-consciousness, or say simply that such a person has attained *moksha,* complete freedom from the conditioning of time, space, and circumstance. The Buddhists call the same state *nirvana,* from *nir-,* "out," and *vana,* "to blow." The ego has been extinguished; there is no more shadow to be mistaken for the real. But nothing appeals to me more deeply than the terms *Atman* and *Purusha* – the Self, the Person within.

Simultaneously, those rare few who discover the Self see the same Self in every other creature. In this sense, life is a kind of cosmic condominium with billions of apartments, each with a different name on the door yet each with the same occupant. This is not mere metaphor. If you knock on twelve doors in a real condominium, the people who greet you are not twelve separate people. They are all the same Self, casting twelve different jiva-shadows. Only because of our physical orientation do we believe that because these shadows are separate, the inner person must be different too.

Even the passage of time illustrates this. At four months of age, most of us had no teeth and very little hair. By four years we have plenty of both. At forty we have a wholly different set of teeth, and all too often the hair is beginning to go again. Are those three different people? In a sense they are, yet no one would say so; we would not be deceived by these changes in appearance. The Buddha would say, "That is not the same person, but neither is it someone different." The jiva is a process, never the same. Similarly, you and

I are not separate, though we wear different clothes, spoke our first words in different languages, and have different sets of parents. One shadow calls itself Romeo, the other Paris, but the Self just watches and smiles. "I'm the only one there is," he says. "What's all the quarreling about?"

This has very practical implications for the law of karma. Once they hear about this law, there are people who want to go all the way back to Topeka, hunt up someone they haven't seen for twenty or thirty years, and say, "Remember the time I threw an eraser at you in Miss Thistlewaite's class? I've come to make amends." The other party will say, "What are you talking about?" This sort of thing is not necessary, for the simple reason that all of us are one. If Romeo, say, has caused a lot of grief to Rosaline, he does not have to say goodbye to Juliet for a couple of weeks and go back to patch up his previous relationship. The same Self is in Juliet too, and the best way he can make up whatever mistakes he may have made in the past is to repair his relationships in the present. Then his way of thinking is changed, and the web of karma ensures that not only Juliet but Rosaline too will share in the benefits.

Yama tells Nachiketa, "Know One, know all." To know others, you do not have to go and knock on billions of separate doors. Once you have seen your Self, you have seen the Self in all. It makes it easy to understand and to forgive, and very difficult to quarrel.

Today a friend took me to a bakery to show me what Christmas cookies look like. There were dozens of them, all cut from the same dough – some in the shape of bells, others looking like Santa Clauses or trees or Christmas ornaments. While we were standing there a little girl came out of the store with her mother, complaining at every step. "Mommy, I don't *want* a bell! I only want a tree!"

Often, that is all that getting annoyed with someone amounts to: "I don't want a bell, I want a tree!" All of us are cut from the same undifferentiated consciousness, the same chitta. The decorations may be different, but the stuff we are made of is the same.

The natural state of chitta is still, unbroken, without any beginning or end. There are not separate patches of consciousness – a little island that is me here, a little island that is you over there. Chitta is one and unbroken; it extends through all. We are only locations on the same endless consciousness which extends throughout life without a break, which has always been and will always be.

The Pauper and the Prince

"If this is my real Self," people often ask, "why am I not aware of it? Why does it have to be hidden away in this 'cave of the heart'?" That is a very reasonable question, which can be answered in terms of how the mind functions. The mind is a process, always changing. Therefore it cannot be aware of anything that does not move or change. The senses cannot perceive the changeless, the mind is bored by it and falls asleep, and the intellect just scoffs in disbelief.

The other day I ran across an amusing illustration of this in an unexpected place: a description of how a frog sees. It seems that when a frog on the river bank is gazing into the water, it can only see what moves. While the wind ruffles the water, the frog sees its surface; if the wind stops, the water no longer registers on the frog's mind. Similarly, as long as a minnow is darting around in the pond, the frog's eyes can follow it everywhere. But the instant the minnow stops, it disappears. As far as the frog is concerned, that minnow has slipped away into another world – until it flicks its tail again.

That is exactly how the mind functions. As long as there is duality – someone perceiving and something being perceived, someone thinking and something being thought – the intellect can follow what is going on. But when it looks at the Self, it doesn't see anything at all. The Self is right under its nose, but the intellect cannot know it. Worse, it does not usually say "from my point of view" or "as near as I can tell." It simply asserts, "There's no such animal!" And there is no point in arguing. All we can do is put senses, mind, and intellect quietly to sleep. In their slumber, as John of the Cross says, we merge completely in the Self – fully awake, yet beyond any sense of duality.

On the other hand, as long as we are looking at the world through the whirring process that is the mind, the mind is all we see. We may think we are observing the world outside, but we are not; what we see, taste, smell, hear, and even touch is the mind-process itself. As one prominent scientist puts it, we never really experience the world around us; all we encounter is our own nervous system. I would put it more practically: we do not see life as it is; we see it as we are.

Look at what this does to relationships. Most of us never really see the people we live with. Our boyfriend may be right before our eyes, but we do not see him. We see our idea of him, a little model we have made in chitta, and on that we pronounce our judgments. To me it seems quite unfair. The mind takes some exaggerated impressions, memories, hopes, and insecurities, draws a quick caricature like one of those sidewalk cartoonists, and then turns up its nose. The person in question should retort, "That's not me; that's your caricature of me. If you don't like it, you don't like your own mind."

This lends itself to comedy easily. When I talk to you, I am really talking to my *idea* of you, my particular marionette. I talk to this marionette, you hear the words, and you reply to your marionette of me. What wouldn't Gilbert and Sullivan make of it? You and your date are out together, everything is going smoothly, and then suddenly the curtain goes up. One person says casually, "You know, I fail to understand why you promised such and such at the Bijou the other night, when you knew perfectly well you weren't going to do it." And the other retorts, "That wasn't the Bijou, that was the Palace!" Each person is in a separate play. She is talking to herself; he is talking to himself.

When we quarrel like this with someone, the worst thing we can do is avoid him. We are trying to avoid an image in the mind, which cannot be done. To heal our relationship, we have to do just the opposite of what conditioning demands: move closer to people we do not like, learn to work with them without friction. When we do this, we are remaking the images in our mind – which means we are literally remaking the world in which we live.

For these forms in chitta are not less real than the objects outside us. We experience the forms, not the objects themselves. Someone who keeps thinking about alcohol, for example, has a kind of chitta-still in his mind, where he can make all the liquor he wants. There are no revenuers to stop him, either; that is the karmic danger of it. He can go on distilling all he likes, but chitta is constantly getting more rigid; his obsession is growing stronger. Similarly, the person who is obsessed with money has made his mind into a little printshop, constantly turning out dollar bills. And the man whose thoughts are captured by Miss World actually has a relationship with her in his mind. Just as with the alcoholic, the karma is quite real. If Romeo wants to run away with a real Juliet, he has all sorts of obstacles to help keep his ego down to size. But in a fantasy world, he can do whatever he likes; Juliet is always enthralled. The ego gets a meal ticket, but Romeo's capacity to deal with a real Juliet suffers a serious blow. Ironically, he *does* have a real relationship – in his mind. But it is a relationship with someone who is not at all real, and the deeper he goes into this relationship, the less he is present here and now.

Here the Hindu mystics make a daring leap: our own personality is no less a caricature than our ideas of others. And the conclusion is even more daring. Just as we can remake our relationships by the way we think, we can remake ourselves.

Take the example of Saint Francis of Assisi, who was so utterly in love with Jesus the Christ that he thought about him constantly. He wrote songs about him, dreamt of him, yearned to be united with him, all much more ardently than Romeo ever dwelt on Juliet. Over the years, as we can tell from history, his consciousness must have become filled with the object of his love, so that there was no room for Francis the former troubadour. It is a beautiful illustration of how completely the human personality can be transformed into what it loves.

This is the central principle of meditation: we become what we meditate on. As we think, so we become. In meditation, we take an overriding spiritual ideal and drive it deep into our hearts, until it begins to shape our deepest thoughts and desires. Here again, I like the parallel with the theater. The mind is a kind of "green room," where thoughts put on their makeup and practice their lines. Once they feel ready, up goes the curtain; those thoughts burst into our behavior. When this is repeated over and over, we make ourselves unwillingly into a particular kind of person. But through meditation we can make ourselves into a different kind of person, by getting into the green room and making changes in our thinking. Just as with compulsive thinking, changes in behavior and personality have to follow.

When I say this, most people make the same objection I once made: "If I act angry, it's because I'm an angry person. How can you expect an angry person to act *un*angry? It's absurd."

"All right," I say, "you're an angry person. You don't have to prove it. But don't you like the theater? The smell of greasepaint, your name in lights, the thrill of the crowd on opening night? Wouldn't you like to be a star?"

And someone takes up the challenge. "Sure," says David. "I'd like to be a star."

"Good! I'll give you a part in *The Razor's Edge. You* can play Larry – always detached, always good-natured; everybody likes to be around him."

After all, it is only a part. "Okay," David says grudgingly. "I can do that for three hours. But after that, I'm going to be my old irascible self again."

That is quite all right. As long as he delivers his lines well and doesn't bump into people, he can act; never mind for now how he feels inside.

David signs on at the local repertory theater and plays Larry for three hours, and he is a hit. So every evening there are three hours of being Larry – three hours of patient, detached behavior. After midnight, of course, it may be a different story. David may storm across to the Café Mediterraneum and start reciting Vachel Lindsay from a table top; we do not ask. For three hours every evening, he has a different role.

Then comes summer. Why not have matinees daily? "All right,"

David says. "If everybody around likes to see me in this other role, I'll do it – twice a day, every day."

And gradually the job expands, until he has played Larry so often that he can do it in his sleep. He doesn't have to stop to think, "What would Larry do in this particular situation? How would he feel? What would he say?" He *knows* Larry, right down to the tips of his toes. More than that, everybody identifies him with his new role. It is like a television serial where you have seen the same actor so many times that you do not remember his real name; if you see him at the Oscar presentations, you say, "Look, there's Batman!" But in practical terms, David really has become a different person. Interestingly enough, he is not Larry. He is still David – gentler, more detached, more patient, but still David, the real David. As the Buddha says, "He is not the same, nor is he another."

Not long ago I took some friends who had been meditating with me for many years to a folk music concert in Berkeley. Even after ten years, one of the musicians recognized some familiar faces. After the performance she came up and exclaimed, "Hey, isn't that old David?"

"No, ma'am," I wanted to say, "that is *not* old David. He does not think the same, does not act the same, does not read the same poetry, does not eat the same food. What does he have in common with old David, his social security number? This is new David, King David; the other was a pauper."

If this sounds far-fetched, it is only because we think personality is cast in a rigid mold. The whole secret of personality is that it is a process, and the nature of a process is that it can be changed. For a long time, of course, this will not seem natural at all. When someone is rude to you, you will still seethe inside. It does not matter; at the outset, it is enough to *act* kind. Gradually, through meditation, the seething will subside too.

This does not happen of itself. When someone has offended you and your mind wants to do nothing but rehearse revenge, it can be the fiercest of battles to keep attention on the words of Saint Francis during your meditation. You sit down, the mind starts up the same repetitive complaints, and you want to throw up your hands and say, "What's the use? I'm just the same as ever." But you are not; your personality is still in process. After a great many apparently fruitless tries, the great day will come when you sit down in meditation, fight it out with a negative samskara, and get up with your mind free. I don't think there is any feeling more exhilarating. Then you know that though it may take years, you can free yourself from any conditioned way of thinking, transform any negative trait in personality.

Sometimes people are surprised when I say that this takes years to learn. They are skeptical when they hear it requires effort. "Why should we have to work at it?" they ask. "Why can't we just *be?*"

I reply, "Can you 'just *be*' an Olympic champion?" Nadia Komenici practiced gymnastics hours every day for almost a decade before she won an Olympic gold medal. Nureyev scarcely did anything except dance every day for years to master the art of ballet. But to erase everything negative from your personality, think the thoughts you choose, be free from stress, anxiety, and resentment all twenty-four hours a day — sure, why not do it overnight?

Recently I have been reading Rex Harrison's autobiography, just to see how a man went about becoming a great actor. The next time you see him in *My Fair Lady,* try to remember the story of his first experience of acting. He was sixteen, playing in one of the little theaters in Liverpool, and all he had to do was run across the stage from one wing to the other crying, "Fetch a doctor! Baby! Baby!" When the curtain went up on opening night, he had memorized his lines thoroughly and run up and down across the stage many times. But when you start an acting career, you know, you think the whole play depends upon your part. So he stood anxiously in the wings, and when his cue came he dashed across the stage shouting, "Fetch a baby! Fetch a baby!"

"Doctor!" the director prompted in a whisper. *"Doctor!"*

Whereupon Rex Harrison ran back across in the other direction. "Fetch a baby doctor! Fetch a baby doctor!"

This is how a very fine actor started out. It can give hope to all of us. An actor like Rex Harrison *is* gifted, but the gift is dedication. Drama schools, he says succinctly, only teach you elocution and fencing. You learn to act through hard, hard practice.

In the same way, we can make a finished performance of our lives. There is no need for special costumes; roll out of bed in the morning and you are on stage. If you drop your lines now and then, remember Rex Harrison and his baby doctor: the play will still go on. At last the great day will come when you know experientially that you are not the role but the actor. Then all your actions will be spontaneous, improvised in the round. It is the samskara show that is dull, flat, predictable. When you can play your real Self, every moment is fresh.

People sometimes object, "How hypocritical!" Not at all. Being angry is hypocritical. Our real nature is to be patient, kind, secure; anything else is false to ourselves. In learning to identify with Purusha, we are taking off our jiva-masks and throwing them away.

Chapter Ten
Death and Dreaming

WHEN I SAY that the Self is real and personality only a shadow, it is in a very precise sense of the word "real," succinctly defined by the great South Indian mystic Shankara: "Only that is real which never changes." By this definition nothing in the phenomenal world can be said to have ultimate reality. We are used to seeing wild flowers come up in the spring and die in the early heat of summer. Everything in creation shares this evanescence: "All flesh," the Bible tells us, "is as grass." The universe is a theater of change and death. Even the body is not so much a thing as a process. The cells that make up my body this year are not the cells of twenty years ago: the proteins change completely every few months; the bones vary from hour to hour. The Sanskrit name for the phenomenal world is rigorously accurate: *samsara,* "that which is in ceaseless motion."

This has some unsettling corroborations from physics. The body, for example, is not only not "real," it is not even solid. On the atomic level, most of the body is space. At the center of each atom is a tiny nucleus, made up of particles so elusive that physicists cannot even be sure what is there. Around that nucleus there is a comparatively vast region of space; then, far off, bursts of energy we call electrons, halfway between particles and waves. Less than one billionth of the human body is material; the rest is space. For the ego, it adds up to a most depressing self-image.

If this sounds like a fragile world, how much more fragile is the world of our actual experience! As I said earlier, we never really encounter the world outside us. In the sea of change in which we are immersed, only alterations of a certain kind and magnitude – "light" within a narrow range of frequencies, "sounds" with enough energy to agitate the tympanum of the ear – stimulate five limited senses to pass their electrochemical Morse code to the brain. From this code we draw all our conclusions about the world. Yet even this is too much for us; out of that stream of impulses, the mind selects only a fraction to assemble into the forms in chitta that we actually perceive. Where is the outside world then? "Outer" and "inner" are not real distinctions; they are mostly a matter of linguistic convenience. There is no such thing as an external world by itself, any more than there is an internal world by itself. These two worlds interpenetrate; in fact, both worlds are one. Even to understand the nature of the physical world, we have to study it in relation to the mind and senses which perceive it.

The other day I went for a walk with one of our dogs. In one sense we were walking together, but I could say as truly that we walked in very different worlds. Muka does not see what I see; I do not smell what he smells. If I could get him to describe a poppy by the roadside, it would almost certainly be a very different object – a blob of subtly distinct fragrances, perhaps, associated with a gray, vague visual form. How would we even start to compare notes?

"What?" William Blake exclaims. "When the sun rises, do you not see a round disc of fire somewhat like a guinea? – O no, no, I see an innumerable company of the heavenly host crying *Holy, Holy, Holy* . . ." Which world is real, which vision? Poetry and physics merge. If our eyes were tuned to an infinitely finer scale, we would look at that poppy on a sunny day and see an effulgent dance of subatomic particles, coming and going from physical reality at the very threshold between matter and energy.

Is all that we sense and feel unreal, then? Not at all. The world of the senses *is* real, but it belongs to a lower order of reality, very much as a dream is a lower reality in relation to the waking state. Dream experience is not unreal. If we have an exciting dream, our blood pressure goes up and our body is flooded with adrenaline just as it would be in waking life. The difference is that when we dream, consciousness is withdrawn from the physical level, the senses, into the mind. Time, space, and causality, the limiting factors of the sense-world, are gone; all kinds of absurd things can take place in dreams. But otherwise, in both dreaming and waking, the thoughts and fears and desires that motivate us are the same.

From this perspective, life as it is ordinarily lived is not much different from a long dream, in which all of us are caught. There is little difference between dreaming in your sleep and dreaming while you are awake. I know people who walk in their sleep, talk in their sleep, even write poetry or solve crossword puzzles in their sleep. Similarly, just because we have had three meals and gone with a friend to the movies does not mean that we are awake. All too often, these are a sort of automatic, thoughtless activity on a relative level of reality. The criterion is choice. In a dream we have very little choice over what happens; everything just happens to us. But how much choice do we have in the waking state? Unless we can detach consciousness freely from the senses, all sense-experience has a magnetic attraction that we cannot resist. To be able to call ourselves awake, we should have freedom of choice every moment.

A good friend once tried to argue with this by referring to what he considered the most vivid experience of waking life, sexual union. "If *that* isn't real," he insisted, "what is? It is absurd to call such an intense experience a dream."

I just asked a simple question. "Do you have sexual dreams?"

"Of course."

"Do you experience pleasure in them?"

"Of course."

I did not have to say anything more. This kind of dream is remarkable evidence that even in ordinary experience, we live not in the body so much as in the mind. The Hindu and Buddhist mystics would go to the extent of saying that we do not experience pleasure because we have a body; we have a body in order to experience pleasure. First comes the desire, then the means of satisfying it.

The Last Great Change

There is another very personal implication to this theory of reality. Death too is a process, continuing and ever present. As soon as we were born death was waiting for us in the delivery room, and throughout life he walks with us hand in hand. In its various tissues, parts of the body are dying every moment. But − and this is the essence of Death's message to Nachiketa − we are not involved. True, the jiva dies. The gross and subtle body are subject to change; they will have to be dismantled some day. But we, Purusha, live in a wholly other realm − the land of unity, a land not of shadows but of perpetual light.

We can find this land by tracing back along the route through which the phenomenal world evolved − in other words, by learning to withdraw consciousness at will from the senses and mind into undifferentiated consciousness. This is exactly the skill that we acquire in meditation, over a period of years. But it is strikingly similar to what happens in the process of death too. When death begins to overwhelm the body, consciousness is withdrawn from the physical level, along with the prana that has kept the body functioning. First it is withdrawn from the senses into the mind, at which point the senses all close down − very much as they do when we fall asleep, but now they are closing for the last time in this body. Yet just as when we are asleep and dreaming, the mind is still full of desires and regrets, hopes and fears. If we are attached to sensory experience, it is terribly painful for consciousness to be wrenched away from the objects of sense-perception. Finally, as the body begins to fail, the Self gathers up all prana from the mind and abandons the body completely. In this final consolidation all our consciousness is collected into the "I"-thought, and all desires merge in the deep, underlying desire of our lives.

In sleep, researchers tell us, we pass in and out of two very different stages. One is the state of dreaming. The other is deep sleep, a dreamless state in which, as the Upanishads say, consciousness is withdrawn not only from the body and senses but from the mind as well. Then the mind is completely still, and we rest in the lap of the Self. In other words, even the ego-process is suspended. We cease to be a separate creature, a separate personality. In dreamless sleep, the Upanishads add, a king is not a king nor a pauper poor. No one is old or young, masculine or feminine, educated or ignorant.

Yet when we wake up, we are the same person again. The samskaras, so to speak, have been gathered into the Self; when prana returns to the subtle body, the mind process starts up again, and we pick up our old personality with all its desires and hopes and fears.

In other words – it is a crucial point – we "die" several times every night. The ego is suspended; where are we then? It is much the same when we abandon the physical body at the time of death. Samskaras are withdrawn into the Self; but samskaras are forces, and forces do not die. Like seeds our samskaras germinate again, and life begins to quicken in a new body and mind, one that will be precisely right for fulfilling our desires. Just as when we awaken every morning, we pick up our desires exactly where we left off – not quite the same person, yet not a different one either. As a caterpillar at the end of a blade of grass reaches out to attach itself to the next blade, the Upanishads say, the jiva reaches out as the body dies to take on another body.

When this is understood, the consequences can be frightening. There are people today, for example, who say that the best way to die is in the middle of a pleasant experience. At the height of a gourmet meal, when all the taste buds are shouting in acclamation, the fork should fall from your hand and you should keel over; this is considered to be the perfect end. If someone were to die like that, I have little doubt that next time around, the desire to eat for the sake of eating would play a compulsive role in his or her personality.

Interestingly, for this to happen, the context into which that person is born – parents, siblings, standard of living – all have to be exactly right. Otherwise the overeating samskara could not flourish. Of course, other samskaras need to be accommodated too; it all becomes terribly complicated. But the point is very practical: whatever body we find ourselves in, it is exactly the right body for us to work out our karma and learn to master our desires.

When I returned to India after my first stay in this country, I took back an electric razor. But when I plugged it in on the Blue Mountain, nothing happened; the voltage was not the same. Similarly, the subtle body has to get the right kind of physical body for all the forces of personality to work together. If the current is AC instead of DC, or the voltage one-ten instead of two-twenty, the combination simply will not work. If I may hazard a guess, this is often a major problem with organ transplants. On the gross level, kidneys might look interchangeable. But every kidney is part of a much larger whole than the physical body, in which the subtle body is included. In this perspective, putting in someone else's heart is like trying to make a VW part work in a Toyota.

Just as we choose our body, we choose our country and epoch. The present age, for example, could accurately be called the Age of Anger. Isn't it Leon Trotsky who says that anyone in the twentieth century who wants a quiet life has chosen a wrong time to be born? Everything is angry – media, politics, philosophies, people. For those who have made themselves angry, this is the perfect age. The times *are* provoking; but for that very reason, there is ample opportunity for people to work out their anger samskaras together. In other words, we cannot blame the times we live in; we cannot blame our parents. "All that we are is the result of what we have thought." Whatever mess we may be in, we got ourselves there by our own thinking and acting. But on the other hand, if we got ourselves into a mess, we have the capacity to get ourselves out. If we have made ourselves angry, we can learn to be patient. And if we are born into an angry world, we can do all we can to lessen its violence. The question of blame disappears; the only practical question is how to solve the problems of our times, which is how our personal problems can be solved too.

It makes no difference in practicing the spiritual life whether these ideas are believed, denied, or even understood. We can attain Self-realization whether we believe in one life or in many. But once personality is understood as a process of samskaras, the theory of reincarnation gives a very convincing explanation of death and what happens afterwards. Death really is a kind of sleep, and not at all in a poetic sense. The purpose of both is strikingly similar: "R and R," rest and recuperation. "As a tethered bird," the Upanishads say, "grows tired of flying about in vain and settles down at last on its own perch, so the mind, tired of wandering hither and thither, settles down to rest in the Self in dreamless sleep." It is the same in death. There is a kind of intermediate state between lives – called Bardo, the "in-between" place, in Tibetan Buddhism – in which we get a chance to recover from the fatigue of one life, review our past performance with some detachment, and prepare to enter another life with a new body and a new opportunity to learn from past mistakes. This is one of the most invigorating features of the theory of reincarnation: even if we have not made the best use of our time here, we have another chance. But we do not have to wait for a new life. We have the capacity right now to make a better life for ourselves, by the choices that shape our lives and personality.

Reincarnation is completely compatible with biological evolution. It only adds that there is a vital, continuous lifeline of consciousness running throughout creation. We – the jiva – enter life at the lowest rung of evolution, and pass through more and more complex levels of consciousness until we reach the state optimistically known as *Homo sapiens,* where we have the choice to go against conditioning. Once we attain this state, for better or worse, we can never be put back. Once we gain the capacity – and the responsibility – for choice, we have to learn to use it wisely.

In other words, life is very much like a school. Here we work out our samskaras until we stop repeating the same mistakes and learn, as Meher Baba puts it, that "you and I are not 'we' but one." Some, like Nachiketa, are really in a hurry to graduate. They learn as fast as they can, get their diploma, and often go back to teach others. But we are free to choose our pace. Nobody can promote us except ourselves. If somebody wants to sit in the third grade all his life, the school has to put up with him.

But being in the same grade is less and less pleasant every year. Our friends keep moving on, the lessons get painfully repetitive, and after a while we cannot even fit in the desk any longer; our knees jut into our chins. "Sure," we say, "it's uncomfortable, all right. But we're used to the third grade. We don't want to grow up." But in the end, even if it takes lifetimes, all of us are forced to grow by the karma of our mistakes.

Schools, I imagine, are very much the same all over the world. Everyone knows when finals are coming – in India we call them "terminals" – yet almost everyone postpones. The night before a big exam at the university, you can see the same scene in every window: the same midnight oil being burned, the same furrowed brows, often struck in despair by the same right hand. "If only!" Some start thinking about dropping out, others about joining the army; desperate situations call for desperate measures. And if you see some poor chap dragging along with his head down, with facts and figures and dates still running through his mind, you do not have to ask where he is headed; he is going for his terminal.

That is just where all of us are going. Everybody has a terminal exam to take, and we cannot ask for incomplete. Most painfully, perhaps, we give our own grades; we decide our own fate every day. When we have been kind, we give ourselves an A; when we have been unkind, we get a D or F. The accumulation of all these daily exams, according to the law of karma, determines the result on the finals.

So now is the time to prepare. Do not accumulate any unfavorable karma; do not leave kindness for tomorrow or selflessness for next week. Life is a process; we are shaping it with every thought. Isn't there a saying, "You can't take it with you"? Why work on getting what you can't take with you – money, prestige, possessions, power? The only thing you can take with you is your thoughts – in fact, you cannot leave them behind. Therefore, the Buddha says, work on your thoughts. "As a fletcher carefully makes straight his arrows, the wise man fashions his life."

The Magic of Maya

In a sense, of course, this vast school of creation through which all of us are evolving is a dream school, for its essence is change. But it is a highly creative institution; every individual imagination is given plenty of scope for play.

In my village school we had a drawing master who could never understand why somebody like me, who was rather a bright boy in other subjects, could not draw at all. I would make a picture of a parrot and he would hold it up for everyone to see. "What do you suppose this is?" And one of my classmates in the back would call out, "Caw, caw!" It is an onomatopoeic answer; *kaka* means crow. And everyone would laugh except me.

That is just what we do within the mind, when we arrange billions of sense-impressions into a personal picture and call it the real world. There is a saying in Sanskrit: *"Kaka kaka, pika pika."* A crow is a crow, a nightingale is a nightingale. They may resemble each other at a distance, but once they open their mouths, you immediately know the difference. Similarly, our shadow world is not the bird we think it is. It is a work of art, but not a scientific fact. If most of us end up using the same words in describing our individual pictures, fully convinced that we are talking about the same things, it is because, as Evelyn Underhill puts it with dry British humor, "for practical purposes we have agreed that sanity consists in sharing the hallucinations of our neighbors." Those are well-chosen words. The idea that pleasure brings security is an illusion, and a cruel one at that.

Interestingly enough, the vast majority of us like this shadow world. It is a very comfortable place to live in, perhaps because we have furnished it all ourselves. Very, very few ever develop a thirst for reality; the rest all say, "If this is not real, go ahead, deceive us! We feel at home only when we are deceived." In Sanskrit this cosmic deception is called *maya*, which may be connected with the English word *magic*. When standing in the land of unity we see only the Self; but in the land of duality we see the Self as maya, the whole dynamic pageant of the universe through time and space. Personified, Maya is the cosmic magician, the creative power of the Godhead: "Charmer who will be believed," says Emerson, "by man who thirsts to be deceived."

Maya is a most resourceful sorceress. If you have ever learned any magic, as I did a bit in high school, you know that the secret is to get your audience's attention riveted on your right hand; then you can do anything you like with the left. So Maya comes on the stage with a huge bowlful of chitta – unitary, unbroken consciousness, utterly without mental or physical form. Then she gets us to look somewhere else; and while our attention is diverted, she pulls out a kind of samskara cookie cutter and starts creating what Hindu philosophy calls *nama-rupa*, "name and form" – in our usual terms, mind and matter. In goes the cookie cutter and out of the bowl come you and I and billions of other creatures, in a great swirl of evolution. And we are all amazed. "Where did all that come from?" We are so caught up in the grandness of the spectacle that we forget all about that one big bowl; we cannot believe that all those creatures are one.

This is the very best of magic. It is illusion, yet it is not. We cannot say we were not in that bowl; otherwise, how could we have come out of it? Yet we saw for ourselves that there was nothing inside but nameless stuff.

Here we encounter the real creative power of consciousness. When an inventor makes a new machine, what has he invented? Essentially, not an assemblage of materials but an idea. He has put together a little machine in chitta, of which the physical machine, when he actually constructs it, will be only an objective copy. Similarly, when a developer looks at some rolling hills and sees hundreds of tract homes, the real ecological danger is in his thinking. His desires have already built a little housing development in chitta; if he is prevented from building houses on those particular hills, he will find a way of building them somewhere else. In this sense, the thought is more powerful, more real, than the thing itself. On the positive side, we see the same creative power in the example of Saint Francis, reshaping himself in the image of Jesus the Christ. In the same way, mystics like Shankara and Spinoza say with a tremendous leap of insight, this whole vast universe is drawn in the consciousness of the Lord. This is the power of Maya, the supreme artist, who spread this immense pageant out four billion years ago and sometime hence will dissolve it again into herself.

According to Shankara, this magic of Maya has two aspects. The first is concealment, covering the bowl, where reality is covered from us – hidden away where the senses and mind and intellect cannot get at it. Simultaneously Maya diverts our attention somewhere else and says, "Look, it's out there!" – out in the vast spectacle of the sense-world, away from the Self within. And the Self, always present, is effectively hidden for eons. It is like getting someone to sit at his window and look out all day; if you can hold his head so that all he can do is look out, you can hide something right behind him, in his very own room, and he will never know.

Only, of course, no one holds our heads like this except ourselves. Maya works her magic from within, and her magic wand is our desires. Pleasure is beckoning outside; we cannot look away, and we do not want to. Maya comes and massages our necks with those dainty, tapering fingers, and we wriggle with pleasure. "Oh, Maya, keep it up! We never had it so good." We never notice that she has biceps like the village blacksmith's. When she has been holding our head rigid for many years, or turning our eyes away from reality, we are stuck with a really wry neck; we cannot turn it any other way. And why should we? Everybody around us is in the same condition.

Plato has a story that is strikingly similar to this. All of us, he says, are sitting in a cave looking at shadows cast on the wall; very few ever turn around and tiptoe out into the light of reality. To make the image more modern, let me again bring in the contemporary equivalent of a shadow-show: the movies. Not too long ago, my wife and I sat through *Gone With the Wind*. It is an absorbing film, and we are both Southerners: I from South India, she from Virginia. So for most of the afternoon we must have been in another world – suffering with the characters, sharing their hopes and fears, caught up in the sweep of history. Only after it was over did I remember that it was an afternoon of illusion. No one had suffered on the screen, though we had shared in the suffering we saw. No one had died, though we had grieved.

Life is much like that. We watch the moving shadows the mind casts on the screen, and we get so absorbed that we forget there can be no shadow without light. Without the radiance of the Self, none of the phenomenal world could exist. We impose the qualities of the sense-world – transience, separateness, change, and death – on the eternal, changeless Self; and we attribute the qualities of the Self – joy, fulfillment, compassion, love – to the passing play of the phenomenal world. Shelley puts it beautifully:

> The One remains, the many change and pass;
> Heaven's light forever shines, Earth's shadows fly;
> Life, like a dome of many-colored glass,
> Stains the white radiance of Eternity . . . .

Shankara uses a different image. Imagine, he says, a large clay pot full of water on a sunny day. Four billion jivas, four billion pots, each reflecting the image of the sun. A child, going by appearance, sees four billion little suns. If a pot is broken, the child cries; it has lost one of its suns. "Look up," says Shankara. "Don't keep your eyes on the ground! There is only one sun, the Self, and whether or not there are pots to reflect it, it is always shining."

The Hindu scriptures illustrate this with a haunting story about maya. The main character is a sage named Narada, who is said to live for thousands of years and to wander freely through all the regions of consciousness from heaven to earth. Narada was on very intimate terms with the Lord, here in the form of Krishna, so he could ask him all kinds of questions. And while they were walking, he asked the Lord, "Sir, can you please explain to me the secret of this magic called maya?"

Sri Krishna hesitated, because to understand maya is to understand the whole of life. But Narada was utterly devoted to him, so the Lord replied, "Of course. Let's sit down here in the shade and I shall tell you everything. But first, Narada, it's terribly hot; would you get me a glass of cool water?"

"Right away," Narada promised, and he set out across the fields. The sun beat down, and though he was a good walker, the little line of thatched cottages on the horizon that marked the nearest village seemed no closer as he strode along. The heat grew unbearable. Narada's throat became parched too; he began to think he would ask for two glasses of water, and drink the second himself.

Finally he reached the village and ran to the nearest house. The door opened – and there stood the most beautiful girl he had ever seen. She smiled up at Narada through long, dark lashes, and something happened to him that had never happened before. All he could do was hem and haw. Finally he blurted out, "Will you marry me?" That is the Indian way, you know; you cannot just say, "What are you doing on Saturday night?"

The couple settled down to a life of connubial bliss. After a while, children began to arrive. Narada's became a very animated household. Somebody was always being bathed or dressed; there were meals to get and people to be provided for. And all these things filled up their lives. Narada and his wife became engrossed in their private little world, quietly building their dreams. Years passed. The children grew up, went to school, got married; in time, grand-children arrived. Narada became the patriarch of a great family, respected by the whole village; his lands stretched to the horizon. He and his wife would look at each other fondly and say, "Don't you think being grandparents is the greatest thing on earth?"

Then a great flood came. The village fields became a raging

river, and before Narada's helpless eyes, everything that he loved and lived for – his lands, his cattle, his house, but especially his beloved wife and all their children and grandchildren – were swept away. Of all the village, only he remained. Unable to watch the destruction, Narada fell to his knees and cried for help from the very depths of his heart. "Krishna! *Krishna!*" At once the raging floods disappeared and there was Sri Krishna, standing casually on the fields where they had walked what seemed so many years before. "Narada," the Lord asked gently, "where is my glass of water?"

Death and Immortality

On the vast stage of maya, with reincarnation as the backdrop, the shadowy jiva that identifies with the body is a long lifeline of consciousness running through time. At intervals there are breaks in this line, where death has come and severed consciousness from the body. But the person who has learned to withdraw consciousness at will from the body and mind is not affected by this cosmic surgery. His consciousness is no longer individual; it is universal. For such a person, body and mind are only a kind of jacket. His consciousness is no more ruptured by death than ours is when we take off a jacket at night.

In meditation, if our senses and passions are coming steadily under control, the ego dies a little every day. Whenever we forget ourselves, even for a moment, the shadowy, separate self is gone. Those are moments of immortality right on earth. Stretch them out, still the mind, and that false self is no more. In this very life the jiva will have died; how can it die again? In dying to ourselves, all mystics say, we are born to eternal life.

We might ask, "Where has that jiva gone? Where is the man who made all those mistakes, the child who played the games I played, the woman who suffered and enjoyed?" Yama would reply simply, "What is there to go anywhere?" You have been dreaming you were a pauper; now you wake up and find you are a prince. Where did the pauper go? "Death," says the Compassionate Buddha, "is the temporary end of a temporary phenomenon" – no less, no more.

Shakespeare catches the same spirit in a marvelous speech by Prospero, the great magician of *The Tempest:*

> Be cheerful, sir.
> Our revels now are ended. These our actors,
> As I foretold you, were but spirits, and
> Are melted into air, into thin air.
> And, like the baseless fabric of this vision,
> The cloud-capped towers, the gorgeous palaces,
> The solemn temples, the great globe itself –
> Yea, all which it inherit – shall dissolve
> And like this insubstantial pageant faded,
> Leave not a rack behind. We are such stuff
> As dreams are made on, and our little life
> Is rounded with a sleep.

When we wake up into unity self-will dies forever, pulling its shroud over it. No one mourns that moment. It is a time for great rejoicing, because on that day all agitation dies, all turmoil, all sorrow. "The joy of this state is unending," Shankara says. This is the danger; it is almost irresistible. The most fearful temptation on the spiritual path comes after the goal is attained, when you look back at the race and want nothing more after all your struggle than to bask in the joy of the Self. Quite a few mystics have succumbed to this, West as well as East. They lose all interest in the world; what does anything matter? I belong to the opposite school. Everything matters: health, education, relationships, even recreation. One way the world is senseless; this way it is full of meaning.

People often ask, "If the ego is gone, how can you feel anything at all?" The answer is that for many, a kind of ego does remain. Sri Ramakrishna calls it the "ripe ego": not green but sweet, just waiting to fall from the tree. It remains solely to enable you to go on giving to life. Like a burnt piece of rope, it looks like the real thing; but as soon as you touch it, you discover that the ropishness is all in its appearance. Similarly, the ripe ego is incapable of anger or hatred or any negative feeling. The only motivation of an illumined man or woman is love.

It *is* possible to eliminate the ego completely; it has been done. But without a "ripe ego," it is very difficult to relate to other people, to understand their problems and be tender and helpful, to feel, to laugh, to smile, to weep, to offer support and comfort and inspiration. To me, this is the highest of all possible ideals. It is a great art. We still act, but now we never forget the unity of life beneath its appearance of diversity. We live with one foot at the center of life and one foot at the periphery – "one eye on time," as Eckhart says, "the other on eternity." We grieve deeply whenever someone passes from this stage; but at the same time, we never forget that the Self in that person cannot die. Even for those still caught in maya's magic, death is only an open door, a fresh opportunity to pursue the supreme goal of life and discover their real Self.

When self-will vanishes, love plays within your heart like a perpetual fountain. All you want in life is to give. It is such a constant source of joy that this earth with all its troubles is paradise, "Jerusalem's green land." It is not that you are blind to the problems of the world. Personal suffering is gone, yet when you see others suffering around you, you share their suffering deeply. In the face of this, there have been people who preferred to close their eyes rather than see the extent of tragedy in the world, who chose to close their ears rather than hear others' cries of anguish. The message of the world's great scriptures is just the opposite. The Lord says, "Make your eyes more sensitive, your hearing more acute; I will strengthen your arms" – so that under no circumstances will we need to withdraw from the world or feel that its suffering is more than we can bear. That very sympathy opens immense reserves within. Then we give everything we can to help assuage the sorrow of others, and in that giving is more joy than the world knows.

Chapter Eleven
Waking Up

WE HAVE ALMOST reached the end of our journey. Of the regions of consciousness that surround the Self – body, senses, mind, intellect, ego – all but the last have been crossed. In Ramakrishna's phrase, we are standing outside the lantern with just one pane of clouded glass between us and the light. The Buddha would put it even more simply: we are ready to wake up.

These images are much more than metaphor. In a sense, there *are* two worlds. One is the land of ever-changing phenomena, of birth and death, cause and effect: the world of duality, which all of us believe is our real home. It is not. Our native land is altogether beyond these: a world which is the very source of light and life, beyond all change and therefore beyond death. In this land there is only one inhabitant, the Self.

Read the writings or teachings of any great spiritual figure; this is the theme. From every age and every tradition, we have personal testimony that there is some immensely far realm where death cannot reach. In more scientific language, there is a state of consciousness in which there is no identification with the physical body, no imprisonment in the mind or ego, but only life at its most abundant. Just as high mountains have a timber line above which no trees grow, the peak of consciousness has a nirvana line above which nothing dies. In this realm there is no distinction between mine and yours, his and hers. Everybody's welfare is our welfare; everybody's sorrow is our sorrow.

In entering this realm, we do not leave the physical world behind. The land of the Self is not a physical locality. We live in the state our mind is in, and as long as the thinking process is active, we may pass our lives without ever suspecting there is another realm. But when the mind is completely still, we see all life as whole. We *do* continue to live in the physical world, of course. We eat and sleep, laugh, work, and talk, just as we did before. But consciousness is utterly transformed. We are the same person, yet wholly changed; and similarly, the world we see is very different too.

Once we finally enter the unitive state, our passport is good in both worlds. We can learn to function freely in the world of duality, yet we never forget who we are and where we really live. But the world of duality cannot issue a passport that will take us into what Ramakrishna calls "the land where there is no night." The senses can go part of the way with us, but they quickly pass out from lack of stimulation. The mind can go further, but it cannot live without change any more than a fish can live outside the water. As we get close to the frontier, it lies down and goes to sleep.

This frontier is a chasm. When we look across, we see on the other side no change, no separateness, no time, no cause and effect. The intellect gets terrified and runs. But the ego stays to fight. In a sense, it has been fighting all along; the senses and samskaras have been its mercenaries. But by the time we get to the frontier it is out in the open, fighting for its very life. In this fight, the Gita says, we have only one ally, the will. And we have only one enemy, self-will. The whole of *sadhana,* the path to Self-realization, is one long struggle to unify our desires until the will becomes unbreakable, for a will that is unbreakable is our bridge from separateness into the unitive state. Once this bridge is crossed, the mystics say, the individual will is lost in the divine will.

In every human being this chasm in consciousness is present. It shows itself in vacillation, in a divided will and the multiplicity of desires, in the inability to maintain concentration on a problem or loyalty in a relationship. Everywhere it means conflict: between two desires, between two people, between a hope and a contrary fear, but always at bottom between two warring parts of our own mind.

There is a positive side to this. The very fact that we experience conflict is positive, because it means we have a choice. Without conflict, the selfish person will continue to be selfish. But where there is a sense of conflict, there is hope. Two sides are warring with each other, the selfish and the selfless, and we have the choice of which side to support.

We can talk about this division in consciousness in all sorts of ways. If you like a horizontal picture, it is a tug-of-war between the selfless in us and the selfish. Again, we can call it a struggle between two selves: a higher, permanent Self and a lower, impermanent ego. In terms of physics, it is the war between light and darkness; if you prefer metaphysics, it is wisdom versus ignorance. Whatever the language, unifying this split is a battle. Without exaggeration, the human personality can be called Armageddon, a field where the battle rages for years and years – in fact, from the Hindu and Buddhist perspective, even for lifetimes. If we find this battle difficult, it is good to remember that through most of evolution the field has been almost abandoned. Only towards the end of this great conflict, when we reach the human context, do we even begin to fight back. That is the beginning of sadhana.

Here we are coming slowly to what traditional religious language calls grace. I have no quarrel whatsoever with this word, but it can be misleading when confused with some external power. Grace is real, but it is not outside us. It can be described as a tremendous force in the depths of consciousness which, when we are ready for it, begins to reshape our lives.

This can happen very quietly. For some quite sensitive people, there simply comes a time when they are ready to receive instruction into a higher mode of living. This development does not depend upon education, sex, social standing, race, or any other external characteristic. All of us have a little window into deeper consciousness, and before that window opens, driving questions like those Nachiketa has been asking are of no more than intellectual interest. When the window opens, they suddenly become personal, literally matters of life and death. Sri Ramakrishna has an apt image for this. We are, he says, like chicks in an egg, waiting to be hatched. There is a time for the shell to crack, right when the chick is ready, and until that time nothing will happen.

Often, however – as with Nachiketa – this awakening occurs in a time of crisis. To the majority of human beings, living on the surface of existence, the storms of life are turbulent but superficial. They do throw us into turmoil, but afterwards we continue in the same old direction: tragedy may strike, but we do not learn from it. But there is a rare kind of human being who responds differently. Because their awareness goes deep, a personal crisis can shake the consciousness of such people to the very depths. The turmoil can bring great suffering, physically, emotionally, and spiritually. But after the storm subsides, they have reversed the direction of their lives.

Meister Eckhart speaks of this crisis in terms of God as a cosmic fisherman, angling for eons in the waters of life. As a great lover of all creatures, I have to admit that fishing has always seemed to me a rather cruel non-sport. But when you see people actually engaged in this occupation, sitting there doing nothing for hours on end and perhaps going home with an empty bucket, Eckhart's image is perfect. It is seldom indeed that the Divine Fisherman lands a fish. He comes to the waters of life every morning, baits his hook, throws it in, and waits for a long, long time, but usually he goes home with nothing at all. Even when he gets a nibble, the fish usually slips away. Of a thousand fish in the sea, Yama says, only a few will even see the bait. Of a thousand that see it, only one will nibble. Of a thousand nibblers, only one will really bite.

But once we bite, we are caught. The Lord is a good angler. He plays us out, gives us plenty of line, and we thrash about a good deal trying to get free. It is a terrible image, but an accurate one. The fish is the ego, and this very thrashing sinks the hook deep into its flesh. The resistance and turmoil and agitation that so often come in the first half of sadhana are all part of spiritual growth.

There have been great mystics who caught a glimpse of this hook and tried to swim away, throwing themselves passionately into other pursuits in the hope of being caught by them instead. It is all in vain: once this desire arises, it will relentlessly consume all other desires. The satisfactions of the senses, the intellect, the ego, may still allure. But after a time, they will hold no more attraction than fireflies in the light of a dawning day.

The desire to change the direction of your life is one of the surest signs of grace. For a while you may not know the direction in which to go. But you will know without doubt that the direction you have been going in is wrong, and you will look eagerly all around for someone who can throw light on where to turn. This desire is the Self keeping its eye on you. It has not actually chosen you yet, but of all the millions of fish in the sea, it has noticed you and made a little memo: "Aha! There is Jeff, hungering for something real." It lets down its hook and settles back to see if Jeff is going to bite.

Saint Teresa compares these stages of sadhana to watering a garden. At first, she says — and here you have to imagine the broad, hot plains of Spain — we have to take a bucket, fill it from a deep well a long distance away, carry it back, and water each little plant one by one. On the Blue Mountain I used to see tribal girls going down steep slopes to bring water up again in brass pots on their heads; you can imagine what labor it takes. That is the first stage of sadhana.

But if your sadhana is sincere, there comes a stage when you can trade your bucket for a Persian wheel. A Persian wheel has several buckets affixed around it, and as it turns, water is continually drawn up and emptied into an irrigation canal. You have been doing all you can, so the Self has begun to take you seriously; now it begins to work along with you at a deeper level of consciousness.

Finally, at the very end of sadhana, grace comes like a steady rain. You no longer have to carry water consciously now; it is present in a continuous stream, and you have only to direct the channels through which it flows.

When the desire comes to change your direction in life, the Self does not rush out to the local carpenter and place an order for a Persian wheel. It waits a while to see how long you are willing to take your bucket down in meditation, carry it uphill, and water your okra regularly. Who knows? One day you may slip and fall, skin your knee, and give the whole thing up as a bad job. Or perhaps, when you have almost climbed up to your garden again, the bucket slips from your hand and the water is lost. "Oh, no! Go all the way down that hill again, just to draw up a bucket that might slip and fall? Not for me!" This happens to almost everyone on the spiritual path in the early days: either they fall down or they drop the bucket. And many give up.

Then there is a third problem, even more acute. In spite of your persistence – falling down and picking yourself up again, dropping the bucket and going back down – nothing grows in your garden. It can be terribly dispiriting. You go every day to check: no okra, no eggplant, not even any daisies. Most people start questioning: "What is the point of all this irrigation if I'm not going to get a single eggplant?" It is a natural question.

But there are some who resolve to go on tending their garden even if they get no rewards at all. Every day they bring fresh water, pull out the weeds, and look after everything very carefully. The okra almost seems to say by its absence, "Couldn't you find something more profitable to do?" But they reply stubbornly, "I don't care. Even if it takes a hundred years, I am going to water you until you burst into bloom."

I have had the privilege of guiding thousands of young people in meditation over the last two decades, and all of them have had to go through this particular trial. They take their parents or friends out to their new spiritual garden and proudly show them the fence they have made, the tool shed, the big scarecrow, the neatly labeled rows; and finally someone – usually the father – bursts out, "Well, where are the vegetables?"

"Oh, there aren't any yet. But that's all right. My part of the job is to do my best at watering and weeding."

At this point, many parents withdraw their support. This is understandable on their part. Our part is to put up cheerfully with their banter. Dedication is tested often on the spiritual path, and not to see external results for a long, long time seems to be the story of almost every spiritual aspirant. Actually, though we do not see it, changes are taking place deep within us from the time we learn to meditate. And one day, if we go on watering and weeding faithfully, we will go out confidently expecting to see no results as usual and there will be a little tendril of okra poking up from the ground. Then we know that our work is bearing fruit.

When you see this kind of resolute spirit, patient but sure, you know the Self has put its mark on that person. But it is good to remember that the mark is not indelible. The Self may mark us, but the ego has an eraser. For success we need sustained dedication, continuous effort. This does not mean that we never make mistakes, but that even if we slip again and again, we keep picking ourselves up and going on. As Jesus says, once we set our hands to the plough we should not look back, but persevere until the job is done.

The surest mark of grace is marvelous, almost unimaginable: the desire to go against all selfish desires. Until this begins to happen, you cannot believe it is possible. When a desire comes up with its jaws open, the whole world believes that we have no choice but to put our heads down and say, "Swallow me up." Isn't this the normal, healthy, human response? But after a tremendous spiritual crisis, it can happen that when a great desire comes to gobble us up, a small voice somewhere within says, "Can you stand up to this?"

We look around and rub our ears. "Did I hear right? 'Stand up to it'? You mean, not yield to a desire? I'll be repressed!"

"Not repressed," the voice corrects quietly. "Free. Shall we give it a try?"

This is the turning-point in transformation. In nothing else does the human being dare so much; no other attitude is more revolutionary. Whenever someone stands up to some external danger — climbs an unclimbed peak, flies an ocean, sails around the world on a raft — we burst into applause. If only we knew what daring is required to face and conquer a selfish desire! Every cell in the body stands for an ovation.

The mind is like a garden; there is a lot going on beneath the soil. Thoughts are seeds, and desires are the most fruitful of thoughts. Up to now I have been speaking mostly about the negative side of this, in which we plant a negative thought and go on watering it with our attention — dwelling on it, weaving fantasies around it, ruminating on ways to bring it to fruition. All this takes place beneath the ground, in the unconscious. But one day that thought bursts into the light. We find we have got ourselves into a situation where it is easy to fulfill our desire, and very often we yield. Consciously it seems as if we have suddenly been overcome by an immense desire. But that desire was once a tiny seed, and it has been a long time growing.

But now there is a positive side. We have been sowing positive desires — this is the purpose of meditation — and if we have been watering them carefully and weeding the mind diligently every day, from deep in consciousness a desire to go against all selfish desires has been sending up a little shoot. Even before it bursts into behavior, there are signs that this beneficial force is approaching the conscious level of the mind.

Often these signs come in dreams, where thoughts rehearse before going into action. Once, for example, a friend of mine with a strong eating samskara dreamed she was about to lose control in an ice cream parlor. The waitress was bringing in a huge sundae, and the sinking feeling in my friend's stomach told her she had already lost another battle. But suddenly she heard the mantram reverberating through her consciousness. The waitress tripped, the tray toppled to the floor, and my friend woke up. (A less dramatic friend in a similar situation simply dreamed that she had forgotten her purse and had to leave on an empty stomach.)

The desire to go against desire may come up during the day too, often in little ways. You may start to act on a desire and find that your heart is not in it; you may even be able to laugh at it, which can help a good deal. Or you may have certain internal reservations about plunging into the same old conditioned action, which will slow you down as if you were driving a car with the hand brake on. All these are wonderful developments, which we are not even in a position to appreciate until we experience them. Before our eyes, what we regard as our permanent personality is being gradually transformed.

The Unification of Desires

Running through these changes is one single theme: all our desires are coming together, merging in one intense, wholehearted, undivertible passion for Self-realization. This unification of desire is the very essence of sadhana.

For a long time, often years, we do not really come to grips with our deeper desires. They have been content to sit back and send notes up to the surface of consciousness. But when we finally break through to a deeper level, desires come to our door in person. Then the battle begins in earnest. When we close our eyes in meditation, there are no more distractions about that letter to Aunt Julie or a deadline at work. Almost immediately the doorbell is ringing, and we know it is Mr. Greed.

In the Hindu tradition we express this conflict in a simple saying: "Kama and Rama cannot live in the same house." *Rama* is a name of the Lord that signifies the lasting joy of the Self; *Kama* is greedy, selfish desire.

The Self is very careful about where he sets up house. When we invite him to move in, he wants to see the deed. "Oh, no," we say. "We're not *giving* the place to you. We just want you to take responsibility for it and stay here as much as you can; it will make us very happy."

The Self comes in and looks around with an experienced eye.

Sure enough, in the basement there is a little glass with a toothbrush in it and somebody's tie over the knob of a door. "Is there somebody else here too?"

"Only Kama," we admit with some embarrassment. "I couldn't just turn him out, you know. After all, he used to have the whole house. But I promise, all the rest is yours."

"Thanks," says the Self, "but you had better keep it. Let me know when I can acquire the deed."

This is the central problem in sadhana: Kama simply will not go. He looks so much like a friend, with us through thick and thin; how can we throw him out? If we try to serve him an eviction notice, he looks at us with affectionate eyes and says, "You'd be unhappy without me, old boy. The moment I'm gone, you'll be wishing I were back."

And for a long time it is true. We may tell him to go, but our eyes are begging with a different story. "Kama, please don't leave! Never mind what my mouth says, what my hand does; in my heart I want you to stay."

If we could only say with a whole heart, "Now go" – as the Bible says, "with all our heart and all our mind and all our strength" – Kama would walk out without even looking back. He does not care to stay where he is not wanted. Until then, he just smiles reassuringly. "Don't worry," he says. "I know you like a book. I'll stay as long as you want."

Saint Augustine describes this conflict in one of the most vivid of spiritual autobiographies, the *Confessions*. At the time of which he is writing, he is thirty-one; the twelve-year struggle in his heart has grown so fierce that it threatens to pull him in two. Everything in him cries out for rest, but not for capitulation; he will settle for nothing less than complete fulfillment. "Lord, how can I find rest anywhere else when I am made to rest in thee?"

Yet rest seems impossibly far. "I was bound," he writes with anguish: "not by another man's chains, but by the iron of my own self-will. My desires were in enemy hands, and he had made a chain of it to hold me down." The description is perfect. Compulsive desires *are* chains, much more difficult to break than those of iron. Interestingly, it requires as much effort to make such chains as to break them. The prana that goes into making a negative samskara like resentment is all that is required to make a positive, countervailing samskara like kindness. Each is made in the same way, through repeated thoughts, words, and acts. Why not make a positive samskara and weaken the chains? Nothing prevents it except our desires – and the odd idea that chains are what we really want. And pleasure is such a gossamer, delicate chain, so attractive, so comfortable to wear. "Soft fetters!" the Buddha says – all the stronger for being soft, all the harder to break for seeming so alluring. "Can you break them? There are some who can" – Saint Francis, Saint Teresa, Mahatma Gandhi, and a few dozen others who have dared to take this challenge and win.

"My will had been bent," Augustine continues – bent by the ego; it is not will but self-will."And a will that is bent becomes selfish desire. Desire yielded to becomes habit, and habit not resisted becomes compulsion. With these links joined one to the other . . . a hard, hard bondage held me in its grip. The new will being born in me . . . was not yet strong enough to overcome the old will that had been strengthened by so much use. Thus two wills warred against each other within me – one old, the other new, one physical, the other spiritual – and in their conflict they wasted my spirit." Simple, practical, and profound. The links are the repetition; that is all that makes the chain. If we keep yielding to a desire – once, twice, ten times, a hundred – it becomes a habit. If we do not yield, that too becomes a habit. One habit chains us, the other sets us free. We all have the choice of samskaras; we become what we desire.

Then, with superb psychology, Augustine gives the secret of victory: "I was in both camps, but there was a little more of me on the side I approved than on the side I disapproved . . . for it had become more a matter of unwillingly experiencing my desires than of doing something that I actively wanted."

That is the turning-point. The desire is still there, but he is losing his identification with it; underneath is the desire to go against desire. "It was I who willed and I who was unwilling: it was I. I did not wholly will; I was not wholly unwilling. Therefore I fought with myself and was distracted by myself."

It is not two selves playing tug-of-war with each other. It is one self, sometimes on one side and sometimes on the other. And the strategy is very practical. Little by little, as concentration deepens and your will grows strong, you keep the mind on your side longer and longer. When a desire tries to pull in the opposite direction, you withdraw your attention from that desire; that is bringing its power over to your side. When all desires are pulling in the same direction, the will is unified from top to bottom. That is as far as human effort can reach; we are ready for the climax of sadhana.

Make no mistake: this is a fight from first to last, and it gets fiercer the longer you stay in the ring. But there are tremendous consolations, not the least of which is that as the fight gets fiercer, you get stronger. Just as a runner gets a second wind, you get a second will.

Even after a lot of training, everybody feels a little intimidated when this fight begins in earnest. There you are in Madison Square Garden, and the crowd is roaring for a fight – friends, family, coworkers, neighbors. They may not say so, but they all want in their hearts to see someone win this fight and be free. The referee announces your name: "In this corner, wearing gold trunks, Little David from New Orleans!" Then you look up. There is Goliath clasping the ropes across from you – huge, steely, in perfect shape. And suddenly your knees turn to water.

This is everyone's first reaction. "I didn't know it was going to be like this! I'd rather be in bed." Of course. But there are thousands of people watching now – people who are going to benefit from your life, who are tired of living in frustration, loneliness, and the constant fear of violence, who thirst to see a living example of some better way of life. And Little David says to himself, "The time has come." It has. This is the moment you have been training for, the chance to change yourself. The bell rings, and you move out swinging.

It is going to be a long, hard fight. There are no easy victories like the ones you sometimes see in prize fights, with one wild swing and a K.O. in the first round. If I may say so, you are likely to be thrown against the ropes and hammered hard. Augustine was, Teresa was; so was Mahatma Gandhi. That is when everyone needs a second – an experienced, loving teacher who will block your escape, bring out the alcohol for a rub-down, and say, "Have you been training all this time just to slink away? They're all yelling for you; can't you hear the crowd? Go back in there and knock that samskara to the floor! "

These first few rounds, in fact, are almost comical. You are in the ring with a big, burly samskara, trying your best to land a blow, but for a long time you never even lay a glove on him. Whether it is anger, fear, or lust, even if you try with all your will to banish it from your mind, your efforts will not be of much use. You see the samskara, take a swing, and he is somewhere else. If you swing really hard you can even dislocate a joint or two, which amuses the samskara greatly. Samskaras have a rather low sense of humor, you see, and no sense of honor at all. They have never even heard of the Marquis of Queensberry; they are happy to hit you below the belt, in the back, while you're asleep, whenever they can. You go on swinging until your arm is ready to fall off, and when you stop to rub it, the samskara knocks you to the floor. Muhammad Ali liked to dance around his opponent for a while before he set in to work. That is what samskaras do, dance around saying, "I'm the Greatest. Just try to lay a glove on me!"

After a lot of trying, you finally connect. Then you really become alert. You know now that it is possible to connect; why were the other swings wild? And you begin to observe yourself with acute concentration, like a fighter studying films of previous fights. When you connected with the samskara, what were you doing that was different? How were you standing; how did you swing; where did you strike? And your skill becomes uncanny. When a powerful urge comes and threatens to throw you out of the ring, there is a fierce satisfaction in rolling with the punch and striking back with all the strength you can muster.

It hurts. Afterwards that urge is a little weaker and you are stronger; but I can assure you, your mental fist is going to hurt for a long time. That is the weight of the samskara. And it just takes the blow. "How do you like it, Little David? Hurts, doesn't it? You're hitting *yourself*, you know." But now you are out to win. It is a deep tribute to my own second, my grandmother, that by the time I reached this stage, my desire to fight back was so strong that I did not care how much it hurt. All the aches and pains and fear of it were forgotten; all I cared was that I had finally managed to land a blow. After that it did not matter how much it hurt my fingers; all I wanted was to hit hard.

You go on like this for years. On the one hand, you would not recommend that your friends bet on you. But you go on training. Very few of us, I think, are willing to train continuously. Even for those who are preparing to climb the Himalayas or take the trophy at Wimbledon, the mind usually insists on an escape clause: "Only for a while. After we reach the top, after we win the cup, we get to have a spree." But in sadhana, success goes to those who learn to train twenty-four hours a day. At six in the morning you may be ninety-nine percent spiritual aspirant, full of fire and enthusiasm. Over breakfast you are still going strong. But as the day wears on, resoluteness begins to get anemic. By lunch you are half hero and half victim, and when dinnertime comes the will is flaccid, your prana account is overdrawn, and judgment is conspicuous by its absence. That is why I lay so much stress on *sustained* enthusiasm – the capacity to keep on renewing your dedication, to keep coming up with a second wind and a second will throughout the day.

The Razor's Edge

Yama encourages us in this battle with words that are among the most famous in all of spiritual literature:

Get up! Wake up! Seek the guidance of an
Illumined teacher and realize the Self.
Sharp like a razor's edge is the path,
The sages say, difficult to traverse.

"Wake up!" says the King of Death. "This is the fight for which
you were born. You have been sleeping for four and a half billion
years; isn't it time to wake up? Don't just say 'Okay.' Don't pull the
covers over your head and mutter, 'Just a little while more.' Leap to
your feet and rub the sleep from your eyes!"

"Sharp like a razor's edge is the path." If you have seen a straight
razor, you know why using one requires continuous concentration.
If you let your mind wander, you may end up in intensive care. This
kind of skill is not learned from a book; you ask someone with experience. How much more necessary is a good teacher on the spiritual
path – someone you can trust completely, who knows every foot of
the path and can show you how to guard yourself against every danger.

In the final stages of meditation, I do not think any human being
can make progress without this kind of loving, experienced, utterly
dedicated guidance. When awareness is deep, just when we are getting confident about our progress, we are really put to the test. Circumstances develop in such a way that we have to give up some intense personal attachment. And there is no other way. When we
have gone as far as we can on a particular level of consciousness, we
simply have to let go and jump.

A few years ago, with our children, I was admiring the skill of
some circus trapeze artists. They would take a swing or two to get
momentum; then, at just the right moment, they would let go and
sail through the air to catch hold of another trapeze several yards
away. That is very much like changing levels in consciousness. Our
first idea is usually to keep a tight grip on one trapeze and still try to
jump; all we get for it is whiplash. Or we go on swinging back and
forth expecting someone to toss us a vine, so that we can swing over
like Tarzan. But no vine comes; there is no one to toss it to us. And

finally we have to take a breath, make a good, wide swing, and let go.

While we are on the first trapeze, this is a terrifying prospect. We have something in our hands; if we let go, we think we are losing something. We are not; we are only gaining. All we are letting go of is insecurity, self-will, some tenacious attachments that kept us from making progress. But it is terribly distressing. Physical and emotional suffering is bad enough, but this is worse. The only comparison I can think of is that it is like a welding torch burning away in consciousness; but there are no goggles you can put on, because this torch is not outside. And it bursts into your awareness at the most unexpected hours. When you are asleep you may suddenly wake up with this torch burning away, and the only help available is the mantram. It hurts so much that the very thought of the next application of that torch turns your will to jelly. Yet all your desires are unified now, and there is a little part of you that says timorously, in fear and trembling, "I think I can stand one more attack."

This happens over and over, until suddenly you move into a deeper level of consciousness. You have burned out a number of selfish attachments which were holding you back, and now that they are gone, you begin to understand. "Oh, *this is* what that burning was for: to remove those chains, to set me free." Then, somehow, there is joy beneath that suffering. Like John of the Cross, you have to fall back on poetry and contradiction: "O healing wound, O fire that burns to purify . . . "

To use a cruel simile, these chains have become part of our feeling, thinking, and being. How is it possible to remove something that you believe is part of you, "bone of your bone, flesh of your flesh"? Compulsive desires cannot easily be cast aside by any human being, for the simple reason that we do not want to cast them aside; otherwise they would not be compulsive. And we do not want to cast them aside because they are pleasant. To let go of them we must have a greater desire, something higher to reach out for. "We require," in the words of John of the Cross, "a more ardent fire and a nobler love" – a passionate, deepening desire for Self-realization that finally makes it intolerable to hold on to anything that keeps us from the object of our desire.

In the later stages of meditation, experiences may come which have as their sole purpose this ardent deepening of desire. The annals of mysticism provide countless examples of these brief glimpses of the goal. Here is only one: the testimony of Suso, a fourteenth-century German mystic who describes himself in his autobiography in the third person. While he is alone in the choir with "a heavy trouble weighing on his heart," he is suddenly plunged into absorption so deep that he forgets himself completely. "Then did he see and hear that which no tongue can express": something without shape or substance,

> yet he had of it a joy such as he might have known in the seeing of the shapes and substances of all joyous things. His heart was hungry yet satisfied . . . he could do naught but contemplate this shining brightness; and he altogether forgot himself and all other things. Was it day or night? He knew not. It was, as it were, a manifestation of the sweetness of eternal life in the sensations of silence and of rest. Then he said, "If that which I see and feel be not the kingdom of heaven, I know not what it can be: for it is very sure that the endurance of all possible pains were but a poor price to pay for the eternal possession of so great a joy."

This last sentence is the key. Whether romantic or spiritual, love does not barter. I once saw a film of which only one line stuck in my mind: "For some things in life you do not ask the price." If that is true for a few weeks' romance, how much more so for the fulfillment of all desires – not just for ten minutes or three weeks, but forever? From my own experience, I can testify that if I had known at the outset of sadhana how much joy there is in the unitive state, I would have cast away all my selfish attachments without hesitation. But in that case it would not have been sadhana. It would have been the stock market: "You give me this, I'll give up that." Just as in love, you cannot set conditions in sadhana. Otherwise these experiences cannot come; your heart is still pulling in different directions.

Closing the Circle

In these last stages of sadhana, we are trying to keep consciousness in a continuous, unbroken channel. The morning and evening periods of meditation set the standard; then we try to extend these periods of one-pointed attention through the rest of the day. While we are working at something, we give the job our complete attention. And the minute the job is over, we start the mantram. Attention must become one smooth-flowing stream from morning to night and through the night until morning again. In a sense, it is like taking two ends of consciousness and trying to bring them together into a closed circle, so that there is no leakage of prana at all.

At the beginning of sadhana, this may not seem like much of an achievement. We have hold of about ten degrees of the circle, so we have no idea of what it means to close the other three hundred fifty degrees. But as the ends of the circle get closer, it is like trying to close floodgates against a powerful river. A student of physics will tell you that the smaller the opening across a river, the faster the water flows through. It is the same in consciousness. All the thoughts that could not get our attention while we were meditating or repeating the mantram, all twenty-four hours worth of them, are just waiting to rush in if we give them an opening.

Last to be closed are the hours of nighttime. As you begin to wake up inside, it is only natural to find yourself wakeful for hours while you lie in bed at night. These are terribly critical times, for there is very little to do to keep the mind engaged. To keep attention from wandering, all you have to hang on to is the mantram. And the fight is on.

At this stage, concentration is really deep. For five, ten, fifteen minutes you stand inside a kind of magic circle: your mind is absorbed in the mantram, so no other thought can come in. But then you become aware of all kinds of other thoughts outside, skulking around and trying to tempt you out. It is a tantalizing scene. One of the beautiful paintings in the caves of Ajanta depicts the Buddha seated quietly in meditation while Mara the Tempter dances around him with his voluptuous daughters and his army of demons. Most people would find this a fanciful painting – very quaint, very colorful, but born of the imagination. In the second half of sadhana, you will testify that the scene is all too real. As Sri Aurobindo explains it, Maya sees that you are about to escape from her forever, and she tries everything in her power to hold you close in her embrace. Great saints may endure great temptations like this; smaller people like us will have smaller ones. But all of us will be tested to the full measure of our capacity. To everyone these tests must come.

As long as you cling to the mantram, all that these fierce distractions can do is dance around and try to tempt you out. "Come on, Nachiketa, just step outside. Elephants, chariots, dancing girls with eternal youth – you don't have to choose; you can have them all." But anyone can get drawn outside by all this hullabaloo; and once you get outside, your samskaras will beat you up. They cannot finish you off, but they will pummel all the prana out of you, rob you of your security, and run away, leaving you with a sinking heart. But on the other hand, there is no need to feel panicky when seductive distractions come; they are an essential part of the drama. You cannot say, "I don't want that Iago on the stage"; if there were no villain, the play could not be acted. All you can do is cling to the mantram and not let your mind even flicker to these thoughts. Grit your teeth and let them caper all they like. Eventually, if you do not give them an audience, they will get tired and go away.

Even in sleep this struggle goes on. Then it is like shadow-boxing in a world of shadows. You are deep in the unconscious, which is terra incognita for the will. Yet you have to learn to wake up even in the unconscious; the whole of the mind must be flooded with light. This usually happens in stages. When you are sunk in sleep, part of you is awake with a little will, and that part tries to repeat the mantram. Sometimes you cannot even remember it. There is something you are supposed to be doing, but you cannot think what it is; or if you remember the *Ra-,* you cannot remember the *-ma.*

As you can see, I am not trying to disguise what a challenge this is. But even at this stage there are rewards. For one, you may suddenly hear what mystics call the "cosmic sound," for which the nearest approximation in sensory sound is the word *Om.* You cannot anticipate it or bring it on, but suddenly you will hear this sound rolling through consciousness, not drowning but absorbing all other sounds. It is such a tremendous experience that Saint Francis says if it had gone on longer, so sweet was the joy of it that his body would have melted away.

If all this seems agonizing, it is the most delicious agony in sadhana. Words cannot describe these experiences. They are so far beyond the realm of everyday thought and sensation that in both East and West, aspirants fall back here on poetry and the language of a lover to his or her Beloved. In these last stages, the Sufis say, all veils but one have fallen from the object of our desire. We can make out the eyes of the Beloved, the hair, the smile, but nothing clearly, and all other desires are consumed in the overwhelming longing to tear that last veil aside. Every day there is this delightful pain of separation, this impatient patience. You expect the veil to fall that very evening, yet you are prepared to wait another day more. Mystics everywhere speak this way, and scholars just throw up their hands and leave. They want rational talk and all they get is contradiction. It is not that mystics are inadequate when it comes to logic; the inadequacy is in language. Give them a language that embraces opposites, that transcends the senses; then they will express all this. Otherwise words have to fail.

All sorts of signs come now that the end of your years of searching is very near. It is like waiting for the curtain to go up on a play for which you have been waiting a hundred years. You are seated in the front row, the theater is full; now the lights are dimmed and everyone falls still in breathless anticipation. Behind the curtain you can see tantalizing glimpses: props being adjusted, the last-minute movements of stagehands, a ripple of the heavy draperies as someone brushes by. Every morning in meditation, every evening as you fall asleep, it is as if the whole universe is waiting for the play to begin at last.

And finally, just when you do not expect it, the curtain rises and you are lifted out of time into the unitive state, beyond change, beyond death.

Chapter Twelve
The Lesson of the Lilac

I BEGAN WITH A STORY; now I should like to end with one. It is not so different from the story of Nachiketa, but this is not only myth, it is also history.

When the Compassionate Buddha was born, it is said, a sage predicted to his father, King Suddhodana, that the boy would one day conquer the world. But the signs were uncertain. Either he would become a great emperor, or he would someday see the suffering and transiency of life and forsake the world to win the Eternal. Suddhodana named him Siddhartha, "he who has attained his goal."

But the king was terribly attached to his son, and the uncertain outcome of the prophecy haunted him day and night. For more than sixteen years he kept the boy isolated in special palaces where every need was provided for, so that he never had occasion to see the world outside or encounter suffering or death. He entered manhood healthy and strong and handsome, with a beautiful wife and a kingdom at his fingertips. Life and youth must have seemed everlasting to him, and all things within his power to attain.

Then one day the young prince announced a desire to see a little of his kingdom. His father, apprehensive, ordered that all the sick, aged, and dying be kept from the streets that day, and the prince's chariot was surrounded by adoring subjects who strewed the ground with flowers. But despite all precautions, the Buddha-to-be suddenly encountered an old man bent and faltering, his body consumed by age.

The sight seared his consciousness. "Channa," he asked his charioteer in pity, "what has happened to this man?"

"That is old age," Channa replied. "It must come to all."

"Even to my wife? My newborn son?"

"To all."

The next day Siddhartha went out again. This time he encountered a man in the agony of severe illness. "Channa," he asked again, "does this too happen to all?" And Channa answered, "To all. As the body grows older, it cannot escape decay."

The next day brought him to a funeral. For the first time, he saw a dead body laid on the funeral pyre. "Yes, sire, this too happens to all. When the body ages, death has to come."

It was as if a bomb had burst in the young prince's mind. He saw now a very different world, where everything that had come into existence was in the process of passing away. Before his eyes, the biographers tell us, every face seemed to change as if through the acceleration of time. He saw the young wither and turn old; he saw the old as dead. And he looked around at his father's court, occupying themselves with games and music and gossip, and exclaimed with the simplicity of a child: "How strong you must be! Even knowing that old age and death are waiting, you can keep your minds on pleasures that come and go almost in a moment."

On the fourth day, the story continues, the prince saw a different sight: a man absorbed in meditation. "He is seeking the Eternal," Channa explained, "that which they say is beyond all change and sorrow." The Buddha-to-be returned to his palace, and that very night, while the city slept, he quietly set out on a seven-year search for the answer to one burning question: *Is there no way to go beyond death?*

If we could live for a thousand years, this question might not be so urgent. We could spend a hundred years playing with stocks and bonds, pursue pleasure until our three hundredth birthday; after we had grown tired of the hollowness of our lives, we would still have time and energy enough to change our way of living. But the tragedy is that there is very little time for experimentation.

Outside my window there is a lilac bush, which I see every morning at breakfast. I don't think I ever saw a lilac until I came to this country. I used to ask my English teacher, who happened to be my uncle, "What is this 'lilac'?" He would just shrug and say, "How should I know?"

Now the lilac has become one of my favorite flowers. A few months ago I had only to open the window to smell its heady perfume, and for two or three weeks it was in opulent blossom. Then one day I noticed that the blossoms had shriveled and died; their fragrance no longer filled the air. How quickly it was over! For me it was not a lesson in horticulture; it was an urgent, personal message: "Everything passes. You haven't got much time."

In South India we used to get this kind of reminder every year in a particularly vivid way. After the onset of the monsoon rains, the sky is blackened by thousands on thousands of monsoon moths. They come like locusts in a biblical plague; you can scarcely yawn without getting one in your mouth. Then, suddenly, they are gone. Their lives are spent in just two or three hours. But while they live they are a terrible nuisance; and when the evening sky is so full of these moths that people cannot eat or sleep in peace, huge bonfires are lit, and these pitiful creatures pour themselves by the thousands into the flames. Even a couple of hours is too long for them; they must plunge into the first fire they see.

Look at the idea these moths must have of time! They do not want a calendar; they would say, "What's the use? What is this 'month'? Life is over in two and a half hours. Give us a calendar for one hundred and fifty minutes to last us from birth to death." Every second would count terribly; a fraction of a second would be a day. If we could tell them that we live hundreds of thousands of times longer, they would not be able to grasp the scope of it. Yet from a cosmic vantage point our bodies are no more eternal than these moths, which come and go in a matter of hours.

We are shocked when we hear that someone with a terminal illness has only two more years to live. We say to ourselves, "If I had only two years, what would I do with the rest of my life?" It is a sharp commentary on the shortness of our perspective. What if we were told that we had only twenty more years? As the Buddha would put it, life itself is a terminal condition, and whether we have two more years or twenty is only a matter of degree. The essential questions are still the same: Is there a purpose to life? What is the meaning of death?

"In the Midst of Life"

In the Mahabharata, one of India's two great epics, the five Pandava brothers go one by one to a lake for water. As each man bends to drink, he hears a voice:

"Wait, my child. First answer my questions; then you may drink." But the men are parched with thirst. The first four who go each ignore the voice, raise water to their lips, and fall lifeless to the ground. Only the fifth, Yudhishthira, stops to grieve over his brothers and answer the questions; and in the end, the others are returned to life.

Most of these questions would be familiar to any folklorist. But one of them has haunted me ever since I first heard this story from my grandmother's lips: "Of all things in life, what is the most amazing?" Yudhishthira answers, "That a man, seeing others die all around him, never thinks that he will die."

In our modern civilization, this may not be so surprising. We have developed all sorts of ways to shield ourselves from death and old age, much as King Suddhodana tried to shield his son. But in the little village where I grew up, death and dying are woven into the texture of life. People know each other, work together, see each other regularly at school or the temple or the bazaar, and it is not uncommon to hear that someone you had played with or whose mango tree you used to rob has suddenly passed from this life. It used to trouble me greatly. Like Nachiketa, I would ask my granny, "Where is my playmate now? Yesterday he was alive like us; today there is nothing but a body. Has he gone somewhere else, or has he just vanished, like smoke after a fire?"

Questions like these became more and more oppressive, and my granny did nothing to quieten them. What she did was immensely more valuable. She showed me a window opening beyond every-day existence and told me, "Look. You have good eyes. If you look far, far off, you'll see Yama waiting for you, just as he is waiting for us all."

This was not done in words. Granny seldom tried to explain her-self; she taught me about death in ways that were much more vivid. In those days my ancestral family numbered more than a hundred, so Death was a not infrequent visitor. And when someone in the family died, the body was laid in a special room called the Dark Room, used for no other purpose. Not even the men in my family would walk past that room at night; as far as most of us were con-cerned, Yama actually lived there. It was my granny who kept vigil with the body in the Dark Room overnight, tending the flickering little oil lamp so that it would not go out. Her example seemed to say, "What's there to fear? This is not the person we loved; it's no more than an old coat."

The next day the body would be taken to the southern courtyard to be cremated, amid heartbreaking wails from the whole family, men, women, and children, perhaps a hundred voices. It almost made my heart stop, especially the children; those cries still echo in my ears. Then Granny would put her hand on my shoulder and tell my uncle, "Now take him to the funeral pyre." And while most of the other children stayed inside, I had to go and observe the most frightening scenes I have witnessed in my life.

No one else in the family understood this, least of all me. Most of them must have thought it cruel to expose a small child to such terror and such sorrow. Only after I took to meditation did I realize that my teacher loved me so much that she wanted me to focus all my life around one driving desire: not to make a million dollars or travel to the moon or win the Nobel Prize, but to cut the nexus of identification with the body and overcome death in this very life. Every morning when I was growing up she used to come home from the temple, put a fresh blossom from the morning's worship behind my ear, and say with words that I now know must have come from the very depths of her consciousness, "May you be like Markandeya!" Markandeya is a teenager in the Hindu scriptures who, like Nachiketa, passed beyond the reach of death.

Everyone else seemed to be able to forget those scenes. I could not forget; I can never forget. Even today, the sight of a little bird lying dead on the road opens up for me a kind of theater, in which all of us are on the stage. Life is a magic show, over so soon. Merely from the fact that there is a first act, you know there will be a last. Fortunes will rise and fall, people will laugh, quarrel, love, and weep, but in the end, the curtain has to fall. It is not a pleasant picture, but it throws everything into sharp perspective. There is not time enough in life to spend on quarreling. There is no time to waste on hostility or misunderstanding.

At this very moment the messengers of Death are on their way with a letter for each of us, posted the instant we were conceived. This letter is not sent by some outside power. Death is a force within us, within everything that lives. We have posted this letter ourselves, simply by coming into this life. And we never know when it will arrive. For some it takes a long time to reach its destination; for others it comes by special delivery at midnight. But the letter is on its way, and every gray hair is a postcard to remind us.

For death is not an event; it is a process. As the Book of Common Prayer tells us, "In the midst of life we are in death." These reminders of mortality are reporting the course of a battle that has been in progress on the cellular level since the moment we were conceived, when life and death began together. A gray hair comes to report that one small portion of the field has fallen. And time is on the other side. As we enter our thirties or forties, the pace of life seems to accelerate. The reminders become more frequent, more difficult to ignore.

I must admit that I for one did not know how to read these reminders. I do not want you to think that I went to the mirror, saw my first gray hair, and said, "Aha! That is a note I wrote to myself; now it has come back to me." Not at all. I did what millions of people have done before me, and will doubtless do since: I pulled it out. Nobody else had seen it; I got it just in time.

But the messages go on. The next gray hair comes on the back of your head, and somebody else sees it first. That is a little more serious, but you know what to do: you pull that out too.

Then one more here, three more there. Sooner or later, you have to answer a simple question: how many can you pull out? Eventually there will be more hairs to pull than you can leave.

There is nothing tragic about this. Youth is passing, and with it the pleasures of youth; these messages come to remind us that it is time to move on to another stage of life. What is tragic is trying to stay behind. To me, there is no stronger comment on the physical orientation of our times than men and women in the afternoon of their lives still thinking of life in terms of pleasure, clinging to youth once youth has gone: talking like teenagers, dressing as if they were still twenty-two, taking advantage of all the ways in which chemistry and surgery can disguise the marks of age, going in for hobbies and entertainments and diversions whose only purpose is to kill time. The phrase is deadly. Yama would say, "You have finished with all this. Why go through it again and again? The experiments are over; it is time to reflect and learn."

The sooner we can do this, the more easily we can change direction. But for those who will not learn its lessons, life can be a cruel classroom. If we have trouble understanding that the pleasures of the senses are too fleeting to satisfy us, time itself will see that they deliver less and less, as if to prepare us for the day when Yama will come and take it all away.

Recently I have been following the career of one of Europe's most famous cooks, whose strength is her soufflés. That they are her weakness also is attested by a very comfortable figure, which in the last few years has been aggravating some serious medical problems. Now she has had a heart attack, and doctors are telling her she has to change her diet.

To the culinary world, this is a pronouncement worse than death. To me, it only reinforces a clear message from all the body organs: "It's time to change! If you go on like this, we'll have to part company." While the body is young, we can eat a classical ten-course gourmet meal with two or three different wines along the way and still survive a little Benedictine and brandy before going out on the town. But after a while, the bill comes. You sit down to a perfect soufflé with all the trimmings and the stomach throws up its hands. "Sorry, boss, I can't fulfill my responsibilities." The craving is there, but if you indulge it, it doesn't bring pleasure any more; it brings pain. Yet the craving will not leave. For a while, the doctors may offer concessions: one souffle a week, say, one glass of wine every other evening. But the salt has to go, and then the butter, the rich cheeses, the sugar, the liqueurs. . . . And in the end, you sit down and there on the tray to greet you are some sliced bananas and a little bowl of Cream of Rice. If nothing else, it is a most undignified spectacle. The craving is still there, yet the capacity is gone, and when you see someone enjoying what you can no longer have, the mind seethes with resentment and regret.

All of us can substitute our favorite pleasure here. I see letters to "Dear Abby" saying, "I'm only seventy-four; why does this particular satisfaction have to be denied me? Isn't there some discovery by which my glands can be whipped up like a teenager's again?" Abby should reply, "That is the nature of desire." The bigger it gets, the less easily it is satisfied. Gradually our physical capacities go, but desires rage on stronger than ever. Then there is no sense of fulfillment in the latter part of life, no prana with which to strive for a higher goal. We are left with a haunting suspicion that life has slipped through our fingers, and a lot of burning desires that can no longer be fulfilled.

Up to a point, some experimentation with desires is part of our human education. While we are young, we have an ample margin for the mistakes that come so easily when we pursue private, personal goals. But as we grow older, we should learn quickly from these experiments that the satisfactions of the senses and ego are no more lasting than writing on water. "There is no joy in the finite," the Upanishads say; "there is joy only in the Infinite." Like a doll or a toy car, pleasure and profit are playthings which mature people outgrow.

The other day, when I went to the beach for my walk, I saw a middle-aged man scrambling around near the water's edge with a child-sized bucket and shovel. While his little boy watched, he was digging holes and making elaborate marks in the sand. When I returned from the far end of the beach that afternoon he was still there, surrounded by a medieval city made of sand, with walls, turrets, moats, even a couple of drawbridges. The boy had wandered away and was playing happily with other toys, but I don't think his father even noticed. He was too caught up in his private world, hurrying to apply the finishing touches while the incoming tide slid closer and closer to the walls.

The next day, of course, it was all gone. With implacable predictability, the tides of evening and morning had come and swept his work away.

Yet that is not the end. Perhaps today, perhaps tomorrow, I have no doubt that that man will come to the beach again. And when he does, he will still have a choice. There is no need to go on playing with sand castles day after day, life after life, against the rise of the tide.

Modern civilization believes that the purpose of the body is to enjoy pleasure. Hindu and Buddhist mystics put it very differently: because of our desires for pleasure and profit we take on a body over and over again, life after life, through millions of years of evolution. Against the vast backdrop of reincarnation there is no hit and miss in this; it is all precisely governed by the law of karma. As long as personal desires continue, the body will continue; and as long as the body continues, death will continue. When we cease to think of ourselves as separate creatures with separate, personal needs, we break through identification with the body and conquer death – not in some other world, some afterlife, but here and now. Yama tells Nachiketa,

> When all desires that surge in the heart
> Are renounced, the mortal becomes immortal.
> When all the knots that strangle the heart
> Are loosened, the mortal becomes immortal.
> This sums up the teachings of the scriptures.

This is the purpose of life, the culmination of the long journey of evolution. On the physical level, the human body at one end of this journey and a bacterium at the other differ only in degree. If you put a little sugar in their environment, I once read, bacteria will move toward it; put in something they do not like and they will move away. I thought to myself, "How human!" That is the nature of life on the physical level, and there is not much freedom in it. Only the human being has the capacity to defy the conditioning of pleasure and choose not to identify with the body but with the changeless, eternal Self. In this sense, only a few of us – men and women like Francis of Assisi, Teresa of Avila, Thérèse of Lisieux, Sri Ramakrishna – can accurately claim the title of *Homo sapiens*. The rest of us, though we are dressed for the part, have not yet come into the glory of our inheritance.

As long as we identify with the body we are fragments, occupying a limited portion of space and perhaps eighty years in time. But there is a much vaster "I," the Self, compared with which this tiny ego-corner is no more nor less than a prison. Our whole modern way of life is based on the belief that we can enjoy ourselves in this prison, find fulfillment in this prison, leave our mark on posterity in this prison, all because we have leave to walk about for a while in the prison yard and perhaps play a little volleyball. If we could only see how narrow this life is, how petty, how quickly ended, we would concentrate all our effort on escaping from it once and for all. During the second part of life we learn to defy all the selfish desires that human existence is prey to, hundreds of them, through the practice of meditation and the allied disciplines. This is not negating desires; it is unifying them – transforming them from selfish to selfless, from individual to universal. This unification of desires leads to the integration of personality in its full glory. Instead of living just for one person, we live for the welfare of all, for the happiness of all. The partitions of the ego are down. We live in all creatures, which means we live a thousandfold more. Everything is magnified: our sympathy, our sensitivity, our strength, our love, our capacity to give and help and serve. This is not the extinction of personality; it is its perfection. As Saint Francis de Sales puts it, the individual personality merges in the divine, as the light of a star when the sun arises "is ravished into and absorbed in the sun's sovereign light, within which it is happily mingled and allied."

This does not mean that the body is lost. The body remains, but we no longer identify ourselves with it. Physical conditioning has no more sway over us, so we are free to give the body the very best of care: good, nourishing food, plenty of vigorous exercise, adequate rest and recreation. And the body responds with health, resilience, and an inner glow of beauty. The tremendous motivation to contribute to the welfare of the whole world releases vitality for a long, vigorous, victorious life, in which all our deepest desires are fulfilled.

The usual idea is that this is a dull, drab, desireless existence. Just the opposite. It is the man or woman who has mastered desires who really enjoys the innocent pleasures of life. To give a small example, I eat excellent, nutritious food, go to concerts, take every opportunity to see a good play or a tasteful film. When I go to the beach for a long, fast walk, usually taking a few friends and dogs along for company, my mind and body enjoy the exercise and the soothing music of the surf the way a child enjoys ice cream. All these are part of my sadhana, for they enable my body and mind to function smoothly for many years of hard, sustained, selfless work. When all desires are right desires, says the *Theologica Germanica,* "all things are lawful, save one tree and the fruits thereof . . . that is, self-will." Saint Augustine puts it even more simply: "Love; then do as you will." This word *love* is used so commonly today that we have all but forgotten what it means. Because of our physical orientation, we think in terms of one-to-one relationships over candlelight and wine, "dancing cheek to cheek," or sitting together under a swaying palm tree admiring a Caribbean moon. All this is just the shadow of love. We are not made to love only one or two individuals. We have the immense capacity to be in love with everyone, with every creature – not in some abstract way, but as the Buddha says, as a mother loves her only child. It is not that we love our partner or children any less. We love them much more, but now we feel equal love for all.

There is nothing sentimental about this. It is thoroughly practical. Every child becomes your child, each creature part of your family; you take care of the planet just as you would your home. Which of us would eat up all the food in the house, burn the back porch for firewood, dump garbage in the bathtub, spray the rooms with noxious chemicals, and then tell our children, "Whatever is left is yours"? Similarly, those who are in love with creation lead a simple, self-reliant life as trustees of the world's resources, returning to life much more than they take away.

Such a person has really ceased to be an individual. He or she is a lasting beneficial force, whose power to improve the lives of others is in no way diminished when the physical body is shed at the time of death. Saint Francis, to take just one example, cannot be described in the terms of a police report: five foot four, one hundred and twenty pounds, living for forty-three years. That is the container; Francis is a force, affecting our lives today exactly as it did when it was embodied in Assisi. As Yama would put it, though his body may have been in a cave in Umbria, the Self in him could move the hearts and change the lives of men and women all over Europe. Where is the difference between then and now? He is separated from us in time instead of space, but that is all. I feel sure that Francis's guidance is as real to some people today as it was to Brother Giles and Brother Leo – and perhaps more real than some of the realities of everyday life that we take for granted. Or look at a figure much closer to us in time, whom I have seen and heard and walked with, Mahatma Gandhi. Even though he laid down his life more than thirty years ago, the force of nonviolence Gandhi embodied is still at work among us, inspiring us and reassuring us that we do have the capacity to meet the worldwide threat of destruction – not by the love of power, as nations try to do, but by the power of love. The first is the power to destroy; power that is invincible is the power to support and serve.

Only with men and women of this stature do we get a proper measure for our own lives. There is a million times more joy in living for all than in satisfying personal urges, however pleasant. Many, many people, if they could be granted their heart's desire, would say, "I want to retire to the Riviera and really live it up. I want to live on Molokai with the film star of my dreams. I want to play golf all week long, speak French like a native, see the pyramids, complete my collection of antique dolls, see my face on the cover of Time as Woman of the Year." Yama would shake his head. "You are meant for a million times more."

When all our urges merge in the tremendous desire for Self-realization, the fulfillment of that desire floods our hearts with joy. "Take the happiness of a man whose worldly desires are satisfied," the Upanishads tell us. "Let that be one measure of joy. Millions of times greater is the joy that comes when all selfish desires are stilled."

"There is no greater gift than this," Nachiketa tells the King of Death, "and I can have no better teacher than you." In the Hindu tradition, it is said that the Lord is extending the gift of immortality to each of us. But we are holding a few pennies in our hands. I don't know if you have seen infants in this dilemma; it happens at a particular stage of development, when they have learned to grasp but not quite mastered letting go. They have a rattle in one hand, you offer them a toothbrush, and for a while they just look back and forth at the toothbrush, then the rattle, then the toothbrush again. You can almost see the gray matter working: "I want that toothbrush, but how can I take it? My hand is already full."

Similarly, I think, all of us ask for a long while, "What is this gift? How do I know it's real? Give it to me first; then I'll let the pennies go." The Lord only smiles and waits. He can offer the gift, but for us to take it, we have to open our hands. And there comes a time when we want something more than pennies so passionately that we no longer care what it costs. Then we open our hands, and discover that for the pennies we have dropped, we have received an incomparable treasure.

This is never easy. Everyone finds it difficult to let go. The whole question is, how much do we want something more, something that time cannot take away? In my own case, I can testify that I too once took a good deal of pleasure in certain private pastimes, which after all caused no one any harm. When I began to see that to unify my desires I would have to detach myself from these pastimes, for a long time I did not think I would be able to do it. My intellect kept asking, "Is this really necessary? Even if you succeed, won't it be a woeful loss?" I began to let go in earnest the day I realized that no matter what satisfactions I attained, Yama was waiting down the road, ready to take them away. After that, the conquest of death came first, last, and in between; everything else was a distraction. Now nothing is a distraction. I enjoy everything much more than before, for now every facet of my life serves one overriding goal. I have not lost anything; I have only gained.

We are talking here about overcoming death. That is the stake for which we are playing. Petty stakes like pleasure and profit cannot be mentioned in the same breath. And the game is not open for long. The croupier is standing by the tables saying as they do in Monte Carlo, "*Faites vos jeux!* Ladies and gentlemen, place your bets." The wheel spins, hopes rise and fall, and the round is over; Yama reaches out and rakes the counters in. Life is too short to play for nickels and dimes; we are meant to break the bank.

This book was written for men and women with the daring and dedication to break the bank. For those who set their hearts on this loftiest of goals, death is no longer a threat. It is the perfect teacher, whose lesson is the fulfillment of one of the oldest of the world's prayers:

> Lead me from the unreal to the real.
> Lead me from darkness to light.
> Lead me from death to immortality.

The Other Shore

When you break through the surface of awareness in meditation, you may feel as if you have been cast adrift in a shoreless, seething sea – the sea of change, the ocean of birth and death. Only after years of inward traveling, when the senses are closed to the outside world and you are miles deep in consciousness, do you catch sight of a farther shore, beyond change, beyond separateness, beyond death. Suddenly, when the mind is still, the words of the Gita on which you are meditating open up and take you in, and the sound of them reverberates through consciousness as if you have found the pitch to which every cell vibrates:

> You were never born; how can you die?
> You have never suffered change; how can you be changed?
> Unborn, eternal, immutable, immemorial,
> You do not die when the body dies.

When this happens, no matter what the rest of the world may say, you know for certain that you have been born into this sea for no other purpose than to reach its other shore, which is our real home.

Not long ago, walking on the beach one morning after a storm, I was surprised to find the sand littered with creatures not much bigger than an old-fashioned silver dollar. They are called, I am told, velellas, "little sailors," for they have a disklike body that floats on the sea and an upright fin that catches the wind. They go where the wind and currents carry them; they have no other power of motion. And the sail is set; they have no choice of direction. Halfway in evolution between organism and colony, they have no fixed life span. They might have drifted on the ocean for years, with no reason to care which direction they were carried in, until a California squall swept them by the thousands onto the nearest shore. In the water, I thought, they must look beautiful, a miniature blue armada with translucent sails scudding before the wind. Now their fragile bodies covered the beach, and whether they were jellyfish or floating colonies or some even lower order, they had passed from this life.

"So many! I had not thought death had undone so many." Even with such simple creatures the theater of death opens for me. The beach seemed like an Elizabethan stage, where a tragedy is not considered complete until the boards are covered with bodies. But in this drama there was no antagonist. I could not blame the sea; its nature is to move. I could not blame the wind; the winds of change have to blow. And there was no question about their direction: all creatures have the same destination; all are going to the same land. But I thought to myself, "If only they had been able to set that sail!" They could have sailed in the teeth of the wind – against the current of life, as the Buddha says, all the way to a farther shore.

It is our blessing as human beings to have sails that we can set as we choose. No other creature has this capacity; it is our precious legacy. And two great saints from East and West, Sri Ramakrishna and Saint Francis de Sales, encourage us with almost identical words: "Set your sail for the other shore." The wind is blowing; we have no choice but to move. But we have a sail that can be set, and we have testimonies like the Katha Upanishad to give us the goal, the direction, and the charts. The rest is up to us.

Today I went to a hospital. As I walked down the corridors, people were dying – not just the old but the young as well. Some of them might have been born here a few years before; soon their bodies would expire here. How quickly it all passes! Time, Shankara says, is a wheel with three hundred and sixty-five spokes, rolling down our lives. We may run fast or slow, but every body is overtaken by that wheel.

The friend I had come to see was dying of lung cancer. I sat beside her silently, holding her hand and repeating my mantram in my mind, until her body gave up and ceased struggling to breathe. Within a short while it was over. As I walked back along the long corridors, it seemed to me that I was seeing the same scenes that launched the Buddha on his search for the Eternal twenty-five hundred years before. There was disease, of course. There was old age, decrepitude, decay. And there was death, waiting for us all.

I wanted a long, fast walk. Across the street was a vast new shopping center, with covered arcades that offered protection from the summer sun. Inside I saw hundreds of people, old and young, wandering from window to window – looking at things, calculating, longing, buying, unmindful of what was happening on the other side of the street. How easily we can be bought! Nachiketa was offered the fulfillment of all worldly desires; our lives can be purchased with foot-long candy bars, stuffed toys, decorated T-shirts, and video games.

In my grandmother's language, I spent an afternoon with Yama today. He stood in that hospital at the end of a long, long corridor, waiting. Many of those in the hospital beds would reach him soon. The staff, the visitors, the shoppers across the street, probably had farther to go. But in time, everyone had to go down that corridor and meet Death. And there was nothing threatening in his face. "I carry out my function," he seemed to say. "If you choose, you can pass me by."

To me, this is a very personal message. The gift of immortality is not the birthright of just one or two. There is something of Nachiketa in all of us; that is the glory of our human heritage. So his story concludes with a blessing intended for us all:

Nachiketa learned from the King of Death
The whole discipline of meditation.
Freeing himself from all separateness,
He won immortality in the Self.
So blessed is everyone who knows the Self!

May each of us realize that blessing, and live in that presence within us which death can never touch!

A NOTE ON THE TRANSLATION

This translation was made particularly for use in meditation, and is substantially the same as that which appears in *The Upanishads,* translated with an introduction by Eknath Easwaran (Nilgiri Press, 1987). A few Sanskrit words have been retained which are not in the text of *Dialogue with Death.* *Brahman* is the transcendent Reality or Godhead; although impersonal, Brahman is often traditionally considered masculine in relation to the creative power of the Godhead, called Maya or Shakti or the Divine Mother. "*Gandharva* world" and "world of the ancestors" are traditionally considered references to other worlds, "heavens," or planes of existence. It is equally accurate to call them states of awareness, passed through in the course of Self-realization.

The Katha Upanishad

May the Lord protect us both, teacher and student.
May he nourish us both, teacher and student.
May we work together with enthusiasm.
May our study be full and fruitful.
May we love each other always.

OM *shanti shanti shanti*

PART ONE

I

Once, long ago, Vajashravasa gave away his possessions to
gain religious merit. He had a son named Nachiketa who,
though only a boy, was full of faith in the scriptures.
Nachiketa thought when the offerings were made: "What
merit can one obtain by giving away cows that are too old to
give milk?" To help his father understand this, Nachiketa
said: "To whom will you offer me?" He asked this again and
again. "To death I give you!" said his father in anger.

The son thought: "I go, the first of many
Who will die, in the midst of many who
Are dying, on a mission to Yama, King of Death.
See how it was with those who came before,
How it will be with those who are living.

Like corn mortals ripen and fall; like corn
They come up again."

Nachiketa went to Yama's abode, but the King of Death was
not there. He waited three days. When Yama returned, he
heard a voice say:

"When a spiritual guest enters the house,
 Like a bright flame, he must be received well,
With water to wash his feet. Far from wise
Are those who are not hospitable
To such a guest. They will lose all their hopes,
The religious merit they have acquired,
Their sons and their cattle."

YAMA

O spiritual guest, I grant you three boons
To atone for the three inhospitable nights
You have spent in my abode. Ask for three boons,
One for each night.

NACHIKETA

O King of Death, as the first of these boons
Grant that my father's anger be appeased,
So he may recognize me when I return
And receive me with love.

YAMA

                        I grant that your father,
The son of Uddalaka and Aruna,
Will love you as in the past. When he sees you
Released from the jaws of death, he will sleep
Again with a mind at peace.

NACHIKETA

There is no fear at all in heaven; for you
Are not there, neither old age nor death.
Passing beyond hunger and thirst and pain,
All rejoice in the kingdom of heaven.
You know the fire sacrifice that leads to heaven,
O King of Death. I have full faith

In you and ask for instruction. Let this
Be your second boon to me.

YAMA

Yes, I do know, Nachiketa, and shall
Teach you the fire sacrifice that leads
To heaven and sustains the world, that knowledge
Concealed in the heart. Now listen.

THE NARRATOR

Then the King of Death taught Nachiketa how to perform
the fire sacrifice, how to erect the altar for worshipping
the fire from which the universe evolves. When the boy
repeated his instruction, the dread King of Death was well
pleased and said:

YAMA

Let me give you a special boon: this sacrifice
Shall be called by your name, Nachiketa.
Accept from me this many-hued chain too.
Those who have thrice performed this sacrifice,
Realized their unity with father,
Mother, and teacher, and discharged the three duties
Of studying the scriptures, ritual worship,
And giving alms to those in need, rise above
Birth and death. Knowing the god of fire who is
Born of Brahman, they attain perfect peace.
Those who carry out this triple duty
Conscious of its full meaning will shake off
The dread noose of death and transcend sorrow
To enjoy the world of heaven.

Thus have I granted you the second boon,
Nachiketa, the secret of the fire
That leads to heaven. It will have your name.
Ask now, Nachiketa, for the third boon.

NACHIKETA

When a person dies, there arises this doubt:
"He still exists," say some; "he does not,"
Say others. I want you to teach me the truth.
This is my third boon.

The Katha Upanishad

YAMA

This doubt haunted even the gods of old;
For the secret of death is hard to know.
Nachiketa, ask for some other boon
And release me from my promise.

NACHIKETA

This doubt haunted even the gods of old;
For it is hard to know, O Death, as you say.
I can have no greater teacher than you,
And there is no boon equal to this.

YAMA

Ask for sons and grandsons who will live
A hundred years. Ask for herds of cattle,
Elephants and horses, gold and vast land,
And ask to live as long as you desire.
Or, if you can think of anything more
Desirable, ask for that, with wealth and
Long life as well. Nachiketa, be the ruler
Of a great kingdom, and I will give you
The utmost capacity to enjoy
The pleasures of life. Ask for beautiful
Women of loveliness rarely seen on earth,
Riding in chariots, skilled in music,
To attend on you. But Nachiketa,
Don't ask me about the secret of death.

NACHIKETA

These pleasures last but until tomorrow,
And they wear out the vital powers of life.
How fleeting is all life on earth! Therefore
Keep your horses and chariots, dancing
And music, for yourself. Never can mortals
Be made happy by wealth. How can we be
Desirous of wealth when we see your face
And know we cannot live while you are here?
This is the boon I choose and ask you for.

Having approached an immortal like you,
How can I, subject to old age and death,
Ever try to rejoice in a long life

For the sake of the senses' fleeting pleasures?
Dispel this doubt of mine, O King of Death:
Does a person live after death or does he not?
Nachiketa asks for no other boon
Than the secret of this great mystery.

2

Having tested young Nachiketa and found him fit to receive
spiritual instruction, Yama, King of Death, said:

YAMA

The joy of the Atman ever abides,
But not what seems pleasant to the senses.
Both these, differing in their purpose, prompt
Man to action. All is well for those who choose
The joy of the Atman, but they miss
The goal of life who prefer the pleasant.
Perennial joy or passing pleasure?
This is the choice one is to make always.
The wise recognize these two, but not
The ignorant. The first welcome what leads
To abiding joy, though painful at the time.
The latter run, goaded by their senses,
After what seems immediate pleasure.

Well have you renounced these passing pleasures
So dear to the senses, Nachiketa,
And turned your back on the way of the world
Which makes mankind forget the goal of life.
Far apart are wisdom and ignorance.
The first leads one to Self-realization;
The second makes one more and more
Estranged from his real Self. I regard you,
Nachiketa, worthy of instruction,
For passing pleasures tempt you not at all.

Ignorant of their ignorance, yet wise
In their own esteem, these deluded men
Proud of their vain learning go round and round
Like the blind led by the blind. Far beyond
Their eyes, hypnotized by the world of sense,
Opens the way to immortality.

"I am my body; when my body dies,
I die." Living in this superstition
They fall life after life under my sway.

It is but few who hear about the Self.
Fewer still dedicate their lives to its
Realization. Wonderful is the one
Who speaks about the Self; rare are they
Who make it the supreme goal of their lives.
Blessed are they who, through an illumined
Teacher, attain to Self-realization.

The truth of the Self cannot come through one
Who has not realized that he is the Self.
The intellect cannot reveal the Self,
Beyond its duality of subject
And object. They who see themselves in all
And all in them help others through spiritual
Osmosis to realize the Self themselves.
This awakening you have known comes not
Through logic and scholarship, but from
Close association with a realized teacher.
Wise are you, Nachiketa, because you seek
The Self eternal. May we have more
Seekers like you!

NACHIKETA

I know that earthly treasures are transient,
And never can I reach the eternal through them.
Hence have I renounced all my desires for earthly treasures
To win the eternal through your instruction.

YAMA

I spread before your eyes, Nachiketa,
The fulfillment of all worldly desires:
Power to dominate the earth, delights
Celestial gained through religious rites,
Miraculous powers beyond time and space.
These with will and wisdom have you renounced.

The wise, realizing through meditation
The timeless Self, beyond all perception,

Hidden in the cave of the heart,
Leave pain and pleasure far behind.
Those who know they are neither body nor mind
But the immemorial Self, the divine
Principle of existence, find the source
Of all joy and live in joy abiding.
I see the gates of joy are opening
For you, Nachiketa.

NACHIKETA

Teach me of That you see as beyond right
And wrong, cause and effect, past and future.

YAMA

I will give you the Word all the scriptures
Glorify, all spiritual disciplines
Express, to attain which aspirants lead
A life of sense-restraint and self-naughting.
It is OM. This symbol of the Godhead
Is the highest. Realizing it one finds
Complete fulfillment of all one's longings.
It is of the greatest support to all seekers.
Those in whose hearts OM reverberates
Unceasingly are indeed blessed and deeply loved
As one who is the Self.

The all-knowing Self was never born,
Nor will it die. Beyond cause and effect,
This Self is eternal and immutable.
When the body dies, the Self does not die.
If the slayer believes that he can slay
Or the slain believes that he can be slain,
Neither knows the truth. The eternal Self
Slays not, nor is ever slain.

Hidden in the heart of every creature
Exists the Self, subtler than the subtlest,
Greater than the greatest. They go beyond
Sorrow who extinguish their self-will
And behold the glory of the Self
Through the grace of the Lord of Love.

Though one sits in meditation in a
Particular place, the Self within
Can exercise his influence far away.
Though still, he moves everything everywhere.

When the wise realize the Self,
Formless in the midst of forms, changeless
In the midst of change, omnipresent
And supreme, they go beyond sorrow.

The Self cannot be known through study
Of the scriptures, nor through the intellect,
Nor through hearing learned discourses.
He can be attained only by those
Whom the Self chooses. Verily unto them
Does the Self reveal himself.

The Self cannot be known by anyone
Who desists not from unrighteous ways,
Controls not his senses, stills not his mind,
And practices not meditation.
None else can know the omnipresent Self,
Whose glory sweeps away the rituals
Of the priest and the prowess of the warrior
And puts death itself to death.

3

In the secret cave of the heart, two are seated
By life's fountain. The separate ego
Drinks of the sweet and bitter stuff,
Liking the sweet, disliking the bitter,
While the supreme Self drinks sweet and bitter
Neither liking this nor disliking that.
The ego gropes in darkness, while the Self
Lives in light. So declare the illumined sages
And the householders who worship
The sacred fire in the name of the Lord.

May we light the fire of Nachiketa
That burns out the ego and enables us
To pass from fearful fragmentation
To fearless fullness in the changeless whole.

Know the Self as lord of the chariot,
The body as the chariot itself,
The discriminating intellect as charioteer,
And the mind as reins.
The senses, say the wise, are the horses;
Selfish desires are the roads they travel.
When the Self is confused with the body, mind,
And senses, they point out, he seems
To enjoy pleasure and suffer sorrow.

When one lacks discrimination
And his mind is undisciplined, the senses
Run hither and thither like wild horses.
But they obey the rein like trained horses
When one has discrimination and has made
The mind one-pointed. Those who lack
Discrimination, with little control
Over their thoughts and far from pure,
Reach not the pure state of immortality
But wander from death to death; but those who
Have discrimination, with a still mind
And a pure heart, reach journey's end,
Never again to fall into the jaws of Death.
With a discriminating intellect
As charioteer and a trained mind as reins,
They attain the supreme goal of life
To be united with the Lord of Love.

The senses derive from objects of sense perception,
Sense objects from mind, mind from intellect,
And intellect from ego;
Ego from undifferentiated consciousness,
And consciousness from Brahman.
Brahman is the first cause and last refuge.
Brahman, the hidden Self in everyone,
Does not shine forth. He is revealed only
To those who keep their mind one-pointed
On the Lord of Love and thus develop
A superconscious manner of knowing.
Meditation enables them to go
Deeper and deeper into consciousness,

From the world of words to the world of thoughts,
Then beyond thoughts to wisdom in the Self.

Get up! Wake up! Seek the guidance of an
Illumined teacher and realize the Self.
Sharp like a razor's edge, the sages say,
Is the path, difficult to traverse.

The supreme Self is beyond name and form,
Beyond the senses, inexhaustible,
Without beginning, without end, beyond
Time, space, and causality, eternal,
Immutable. Those who realize the Self
Are forever free from the jaws of death.

The wise, who gain experiential knowledge
Of this timeless tale of Nachiketa,
Narrated by Death, attain the glory
Of living in spiritual awareness.
Those who, full of devotion, recite this
Supreme mystery at a spiritual
Gathering, are fit for eternal life.
They are indeed fit for eternal life.

PART TWO

I

The self-existent Lord pierced the senses
To turn outward. Thus we look to the world outside
And see not the Self within us.
A sage withdrew his senses from the world of change
And, seeking immortality,
Looked within and beheld the deathless Self.

The immature run after sense pleasures
And fall into the widespread net of death.
But the wise, knowing the Self as deathless,
Seek not the changeless in the world of change.

That through which one enjoys form, taste, smell, sound,
Touch, and sexual union is the Self.

Can there be anything not known to That
Who is the One in all? Know One, know all.
That through which one enjoys the waking
And sleeping states is the Self. To know That
As consciousness is to go beyond sorrow.

Those who know the Self as enjoyer
Of the honey from the flowers of the senses,
Ever present within, ruler of time,
Go beyond fear. For this Self is supreme!

The god of creation, Brahma,
Born of the Godhead through meditation
Before the waters of life were created,
Who stands in the heart of every creature,
Is the Self indeed. For this Self is supreme!

The goddess of energy, Aditi,
Born of the Godhead through vitality,
Mother of all the cosmic forces
Who stands in the heart of every creature,
Is the Self indeed. For this Self is supreme!

The god of fire, Agni, hidden between
Two firesticks like a child well protected
In the mother's womb, whom we adore
Every day in meditation,
Is the Self indeed. For this Self is supreme!

That which is the source of the sun
And of every power in the cosmos, beyond which
There is neither going nor coming,
Is the Self indeed. For this Self is supreme!

What is here is also there; what is there,
Also here. Who sees multiplicity
But not the one indivisible Self
Must wander on and on from death to death.

Only the one-pointed mind attains
This state of unity. There is no one
But the Self. Who sees multiplicity

But not the one indivisible Self
Must wander on and on from death to death.

That thumb-sized being enshrined in the heart,
Ruler of time, past and future,
To see whom is to go beyond all fear,
Is the Self indeed. For this Self is supreme!

That thumb-sized being, a flame without smoke,
Ruler of time, past and future,
The same on this day as on tomorrow,
Is the Self indeed. For this Self is supreme!

As the rain on a mountain peak runs off
The slopes on all sides, so those who see
Only the seeming multiplicity of life
Run after things on every side.

As pure water poured into pure water
Becomes the very same, so does the Self
Of the illumined man or woman, Nachiketa,
Verily become one with the Godhead.

2

There is a city with eleven gates
Of which the ruler is the unborn Self,
Whose light forever shines. They go beyond
Sorrow who meditate on the Self
And are freed from the cycle of birth and death.
For this Self is supreme!

The Self is the sun shining in the sky,
The wind blowing in space; he is the fire
At the altar and in the home the guest;
He dwells in human beings, in gods, in truth,
And in the vast firmament; he is the fish
Born in water, the plant growing in the earth,
The river flowing down from the mountain.
For this Self is supreme!

The adorable one who is seated
In the heart rules the breath of life.

Unto him all the senses pay their homage.
When the dweller in the body breaks out
In freedom from the bonds of flesh, what remains?
For this Self is supreme!

We live not by the breath that flows in
And flows out, but by him who causes the breath
To flow in and flow out.

Now, O Nachiketa, I will tell you
Of this unseen, eternal Brahman, and
What befalls the Self after death. Of those
Unaware of the Self, some are born as
Embodied creatures while others remain
In a lower stage of evolution,
As determined by their own need for growth.

That which is awake even in our sleep,
Giving form in dreams to the objects of
Sense craving, that indeed is pure light,
Brahman the immortal, who contains all
The cosmos, and beyond whom none can go.
For this Self is supreme!

As the same fire assumes different shapes
When it consumes objects differing in shape,
So does the one Self take the shape
Of every creature in whom he is present.
As the same air assumes different shapes
When it enters objects differing in shape,
So does the one Self take the shape
Of every creature in whom he is present.

As the sun, who is the eye of the world,
Cannot be tainted by the defects in our eyes
Or by the objects it looks on,
So the one Self, dwelling in all, cannot
Be tainted by the evils of the world.
For this Self transcends all!

The ruler supreme, inner Self of all,
Multiplies his oneness into many.

Eternal joy is theirs who see the Self
In their own hearts. To none else does it come!

Changeless amidst the things that pass away,
Pure consciousness in all who are conscious,
The One answers the prayers of many.
Eternal peace is theirs who see the Self
In their own hearts. To none else does it come!

NACHIKETA

How can I know that blissful Self, supreme,
Inexpressible, realized by the wise?
Is he the light, or does he reflect light?

YAMA

There shines not the sun, neither moon nor star,
Nor flash of lightning, nor fire lit on earth.
The Self is the light reflected by all.
He shining, everything shines after him.

3

The Tree of Eternity has its roots above
And its branches on earth below.
Its pure root is Brahman the immortal
From whom all the worlds draw their life, and whom
None can transcend. For this Self is supreme!

The cosmos comes forth from Brahman and moves
In him. With his power it reverberates,
Like thunder crashing in the sky. Those who realize him
Pass beyond the sway of death.

In fear of him fire burns; in fear of him
The sun shines, the clouds rain, and the winds blow.
In fear of him death stalks about to kill.

If one fails to realize Brahman in this life
Before the physical sheath is shed,
He must again put on a body
In the world of embodied creatures.

Brahman can be seen, as in a mirror,
In a pure heart; in the world of the ancestors
As in a dream; in the *gandharva* world
As the reflections in trembling waters;
And clear as light in the realm of Brahma.

Knowing the senses to be separate
From the Self, and the sense experience
To be fleeting, the wise grieve no more.

Above the senses is the mind,
Above the mind is the intellect, above that
Is the ego, and above the ego
Is the unmanifested Cause.
And beyond is Brahman, omnipresent,
Attributeless. Realizing him one is released
From the cycle of birth and death.

He is formless, and can never be seen
With these two eyes. But he reveals himself
In the heart made pure through meditation
And sense-restraint. Realizing him one is released
From the cycle of birth and death.

When the five senses are stilled, when the mind
Is stilled, when the intellect is stilled,
That is called the highest state by the wise.
They say yoga is this complete stillness
In which one enters the unitive state,
Never to become separate again.
If one is not established in this state,
The sense of unity will come and go.

The unitive state cannot be attained
Through words or thoughts or through the eye.
How can it be attained except through one who is
Established in this state himself?

There are two selves, the separate ego
And the indivisible Atman. When

One rises above *I* and *me* and *mine*,
The Atman is revealed as one's real Self.

When all desires that surge in the heart
Are renounced, the mortal becomes immortal.
When all the knots that strangle the heart
Are loosened, the mortal becomes immortal.
This sums up the teaching of the scriptures.

From the heart there radiate a hundred
And one vital tracks. One of them rises
To the crown of the head. This way leads
To immortality, the others to death.

The Lord of Love, not larger than the thumb,
Is ever enshrined in the hearts of all.
Draw him clear out of the physical sheath,
As one draws the stalk from the munja grass.
Know thyself to be pure and immortal!
Know thyself to be pure and immortal!

THE NARRATOR

Nachiketa learned from the King of Death
The whole discipline of meditation.
Freeing himself from all separateness,
He won immortality in Brahman.
So blessed is everyone who knows the Self!

OM *shanti shanti shanti*

Index

Index

Bible, 17, 160, 185
Birth, and reincarnation, 165–166
Blake, William, 146, 161
Body, physical: and mind, see Mind, and body; as chariot, 34, 35; as city, 41–43; as jacket, 173; as process, 160–164; at death, 163–164, 173 (*See also* Reincarnation); care of, 207; fixing attention on, 59–60, 61; Hindu and Buddhist perspective on, 163, 205; identification with, 34, 41, 48–50, 206 (*See also* Appearance, physical; Body-consciousness)
Body, subtle, 56–57, 66, 76–80, 165. *See also* Mind
Body-consciousness, 30, 61, 97 *See also* Body, physical, identification with; Consciousness at death
Book of Common Prayer, 202
Brain, 58, 67
Buddha: on anger, 84; on consequences of actions, 136; on death, 121, 173; on desire, 85, 95, 98, 104, 142; on going against current, 212; on love, 208; on physical change, 151; on thoughts, 142, 168; on self-will, 85, 142; on unity of life, 121; on waking up, 176; seeks the Eternal, 21, 213; story of, 197–199; temptations of, 194
Buddhi, 106
Buddhist mystics. *See* Hindu and Buddhist mystics
Buddhism: law of karma in, 135; mantram in, 130; reincarnation in, 94, 148, 178, 205–206; perspective on body in, 57, 205

Cancer, 75, 118
Cardiovascular disease, 88–89, 90
Catherine of Siena, Saint, 151
Change, 18, 72–74, 149, 153, 160–161, 171–173, 177, 198–199, 211–212. *See also* Death, as process; Mind, as process
Changeless, the, 149, 153, 171, 206
Chitta: defined, 111–113, 124–126, 152–155; forms in, 124, 126, 154, 161; mind and matter created from, 160–162; same in all, 152, 153, 169; state of mind and, 111–

113; thoughts and, 124–126, 155; waves in, 111–112, 126; will and, 113
Choice, 31, 33, 39–44, 81, 87, 90: and desires, 94, 104–105, 182; and karma, 139–140; and prana, 81; and senses, 35, 162; and thinking, 87, 90, 125; and will, 102–103, 104–105, 107; capacity for, 31, 39, 162, 166, 205, 212; conflict and, 178; freedom of, 105, 162; of context for birth, 164–166; of direction in life, 212; of going beyond death, 213; of identifying with Self, 206; of samskaras, 186
Christ-consciousness, 151
City of Eleven Gates, 41–42, 51
Compulsions. *See* Conditioning; Desire, selfish; *Samskaras*
Conditioning, 90–91: and karma, 139; and self-will, 104; going against, 90, 97, 104–105, 130–131, 154, 206; in thinking, 127–128; mantram and, 130. *See also Samskaras*
Confessions (Augustine), 185
Conflict, inner, 178, 184–186
Consciousness, 111–112, 176–179: and evolution, 166; and meditation, 19–20, 30, 120, 150, 163, 183–184; at death, 163, 173; center of, 52; closing circle of, 193; creative power of, 169; depths of, 20, 131, 179; division in, 178; desires and, 183; eternal, 149; expansion of, 120; individual, 173; journey into, 30, 41, 150, 176; levels of, 30, 181, 190–191; physical level of, 41, 150 (*See also* Body-consciousness); stuff of, *see Chitta;* transformation of, 177–179; undifferentiated, 149, 152, 163; universal, 173; window into, 179; withdrawal of, 150, 163, 173
Consequences, 107–109, 119–120, 135–136, 138–139. *See also Karma*
Cosmic sound, 195
Cousins, Norman, 136
Cravings, 45, 93–94, 99, 146. *See also* Desire, selfish
Crisis, 47, 96, 179, 182

Index

Index

Index

Schmale, Arthur, 73
Seeing clearly, 106–112, 119–120
Self, 20, 145–153 passim, 160, 169–
    171, 184–185, 206: and grace,
    180–181, 182; and maya, 145,
    169, 170; and meditation, 20, 30,
    63, 147, 150; as force, 147, 208; as
    observer, 146; as rider, 34–37; as
    ruler, 43; at death, 163–164; con-
    fusing, with phenomenal world,
    170–171; discovering, 20, 31,
    147–148, 150, 153, 159 (See also
    Self-realization); in dreamless
    sleep, 164, 166; inability to per-
    ceive, 153; is same in all, 151–
    152; layers covering, 30; moving
    away from, 148–149, 150; names
    for, 151; realm of, 176–177
Self-realization, 20, 24, 150, 196,
    211: and death, 42–43; desire for,
    24, 179–180, 184, 192–193, 195–
    196, 209; joy of, 174, 209; path to,
    see Sadhana. See also Self, discov-
    ering; Unitive state
Self-will, 104, 141–142, 177–178,
    208: absence of, 142–143, 174–
    175; and karma, 141–142; and
    selfish desires, 104, 141, 185, 186;
    and stress, 85–86; hides Self, 145;
    in marriage, 62
Selye, Hans, 71, 81, 84–85, 89
Senility, 82
Senses: and depression, 45–48; and
    prana, 45, 79; as gates, 43–45; as
    horses, 34–37; at death, 163; and
    change, 153–154; consuming
    through, 43–44, 45; identifying
    with, 44–45, 52–53; power of, 35;
    reality of, 162; training the, 35,
    36, 41, 44 (see also Desire, selfish,
    and will); uncontrolled, 35–39,
    44–46. See also Pleasure
Separateness, 119, 120, 122, 150,
    151: cessation of, 120, 150, 163.
    See also Unity of life
Sex, 23, 47, 50, 62, 83, 88, 94
Shakespeare, 17, 87, 88, 89, 109–
    110, 174
Shankara, 160, 170, 171, 174, 213
Shānti, 142
Shaw, George Bernard, 116
Shelley, Percy Bysshe, 171
Shreya. See Preya and shreya

Sleep: dreaming, 80, 162–164; prana
    in, 80; purpose of, 80, 166; strug-
    gle in, 194–195
Smoking, 33–34, 136, 139–140
Speech, 136, 137
Spinoza, Baruch, 104, 170
Spiritual path. See Sadhana
Sthūla–sharīra, 56
Stimulus and response, 67, 105, 126–
    132, 134, 139. See also Condition-
    ing
Stream of consciousness, 124
Stress: and illness, 64, 71, 76, 84–85,
    89–91; and prana, 81–82; cause of,
    65, 71, 89; drinking to relieve, 62
Subtle body. See Mind
Success, 69, 91, 93, 95, 182, 189
Suffering, 104
Sūkshma–sharīra, 56
Suso, Henry, 192

Taste, 32, 35, 44, 45, 134–135
Teacher, spiritual, 28, 188, 190, 209.
    See also Easwaran's Grandmother;
    Yama, as teacher
Television, 58, 76, 112, 157
Tempest, The (Shakespeare), 174
Teresa of Avila, Saint, 23, 41, 54,
    180–181, 206
Temptations and tests: Nachiketa's,
    24–29; in sadhana, 190, 193–194
Theologica Germanica, 208
Thérèse of Lisieux, Saint, 24, 95
Thinking process, 125–132: and
    chitta, 111–113, 124, 126; and
    karma, 135–138, 141–142; and
    mantram, 130; and meditation,
    126–131; compared to fire works,
    125–126, to game, 127, to movie,
    126–127; mastering, 128, 129–
    130, 132; speed of, 126–127, 128–
    129, 142. See also Mind, as pro-
    cess; Samskaras; Thoughts
Thompson, Francis, 51
Thoughts: and chitta, 111, 124, 126;
    as food for mind, 71–72; changing,
    63, 90–91, 155–156 (See also
    Thinking process, mastering;
    Samskaras, overcoming); choice
    of, 125, 130, 142–143; emotional
    charge of, 126; gap between, 125–
    128; life is shaped by, 71–72, 167–
    168; negative, 65, 71–72, 76,

Index

★ ★ ★

Library of Congress Cataloging-in-Publication Data:

Easwaran, Eknath.
Dialogue with death : a journey into consciousness / by
   Eknath Easwaran – 2nd ed.
       p.   cm.
   ISBN 0–915132–73–7 (alk. paper) : $22.00
   ISBN 0–915132–72–9 (alk. paper) : $13.95
1. Upanishads. Kathopanishad – Criticism, interpretation, etc.
       2. Spiritual life – Hinduism .
   I. Upanishads. Kathopanishad. English.   II. Title.
   BL1124.7.K38E19 1992 294.5'9218 – dc20
                   92–38898